T0334513

Five Centuries of Books and Manuscripts in Modern Greek

A Catalogue of an Exhibition at the Houghton Library

December 4, 1987 through February 17, 1988

EVRO LAYTON

The Harvard College Library

Cambridge, Massachusetts

1990

Designed by Richard C. Bartlett

Composed by Crane Typesetting Service, Inc.

Printed and bound by the Office of the University Publisher, Harvard University

Text and pictures edited by Roger E. Stoddard

Photographs by Victor Santamaria and Dan Sullivan

Front and back covers: factotum from the title page of an *Evangelistarion* (Venice, G. A. Pinelli, 1606)

Inside covers: illustrations from item 21

Introduction

i. Modern Greek literature: difference and diversity

Nikos Demos, in his collection of aphorisms, *The Misfortune of Being Greek* (1975), writes:

> Any people descended from the ancient Greeks would automatically be unhappy. Unless he could forget them, or surpass them.

And again:

> Whenever a Greek speaks of 'Europe,' he automatically excludes Greece. When a foreigner speaks of Europe, we do not entertain the possibility of his not including Greece.

These two questions, the relationship of modern Greece to its past and to Europe, need to be addressed, if the difference and diversity of modern Greek literature are to be fully appreciated.

There can be few literatures so diverse, yet so difficult to define and to date, as that of 'modern' Greece. What does it have to offer, not just to Greeks, but to European and world literatures more generally? Since modern Greek literature followed from the outset a different course from that of Western European literatures, it needs to be viewed with perspectives and criteria other than those evolved largely on the basis of Western experience. In other words, 'difference' should not be treated as a sign of 'belatedness' or 'inferiority', but welcomed as a means for testing the validity of Eurocentric critical assumptions all too frequently allowed to form the basis for universal, archetypal or reductionist theories about literary history.

What, then, is modern Greek literature? When and where does it begin? An historian might have little hesitation in pointing to the Ottoman conquest of Constantinople in 1453 as the demarcation between the Byzantine and modern periods, and to the emergence of the Greek nation-state after the War of Independence (1821–28) as the catalyst for the formation of a distinctively modern Greek consciousness. Yet historical events, however momentous, may prove unreliable indicators of cultural and linguistic change. In the West, the break between medieval and modern literatures —if not quite as clean as is sometimes supposed—can be measured by the emergence and conscious cultivation of the vernacular tongues as distinct from medieval Latin. In the Byzantine East, the linguistic situation was far more fluid and complex, with the result that the medieval past has lived on into the present to a much greater extent than in Western Europe. Although almost all secular literature, at least until the twelfth century, was composed in archaising Greek (that is, attempts to imitate the long defunct Attic Greek of classical antiquity), we know from inscriptions and non-literary papyri of the second through seventh centuries, and from many other non-literary or 'low-style' sources, that spoken and informal forms of the language approximated far more closely to modern than to ancient Greek. As for the New Testament, the Hymns of Romanos the Melodist, and the Orthodox liturgy, they are composed not in archaising Greek but in varying forms of the Hellenistic *koine*—again closer to modern than to ancient Greek, and still readily understood by Greeks of every educational level. All these—and many other—ecclesiastical texts remain a living part of the modern heritage, and to this day are assimilated into modern literary texts, from Dionysios Solomos to Odysseas Elytis and Kostas Tachtsis. Nor should we forget that even though Greek remained during the Byzantine period the major language for written records, other languages and cultures made substantial contributions throughout, from Ephrem the Syrian (fourth century A.D.) through his influence on Romanos the Melodist (himself probably a Hellenised Jew from Emessa in Syria), to Bergadis of Crete, author of the first literary text to be printed in modern Greek, who

—judging from his name—might have been descended from the noble Venetian family of the Bragadin.

If modern Greek literature is to be defined as literature in the modern language (and it is hard to find another objective criterion), then its emergence has to be traced back to the Comnenian court of twelfth-century Constantinople, where the 'vulgar language' was consciously and for the first time creatively cultivated by court poets as a new medium for literary expression. For example, the four so-called Ptochoprodromic Poems, dateable to the late twelfth century and attributed to the versatile and prolific Theodore Prodromos, reveal a critical stance towards established conventions of genre and language on a scale qualitatively comparable to Dante's. Such courtly experimentation with vernacular verse forms was appropriate to the emerging genres of prison and beggar poems, which satirised both the flattery of elaborate 'high-style' court poetry and the ascendant wealth and prestige of the urban artisan classes. It is important to stress that our earliest examples of modern Greek literature are neither populist tracts composed by and for the less educated, nor inferior pieces in second-rate Greek, but sophisticated and highly-wrought poems which mark a new departure with, if anything, an aristocratic message. The well-known tirade 'against learning' in the fourth Prodromic Poem—spoken by the narrating persona, an impoverished scholar—is not an attack on learning, but rather a complaint that a proper education will no longer earn bread, whereas the common artisans, craftsmen and ordinary tradesmen of the City live in unprecedented prosperity:

> Ever since I was a lad, my father used to tell me,
> 'Learn letters, boy, as much as you are able.
> You see that man there, child, he used to walk on foot;
> now he rides a fat mule with double rein-straps;
> While he was learning, he wore no shoes at all;
> and now, look at him, he wears long pointed ones.
> While learning, he never glimpsed the bath-gates;
> but now he takes a bath three times a week.
> His belt-fold used to swell with lice the size of almonds;
> now, it is swell with Manuels's *hyperpyra* [= recently minted gold coins].
> So, be persuaded with your old man's fatherly advice,
> and learn your grammar — as much as you are able.'
> So I learned my grammar, with a great deal of effort.
> Now that I've become, supposedly, a craftsman,
> I lack both bread and even bread-crumb.
> I spit on grammar and I say with tears,
> 'Christ, down with letters, and with whoever wants them!
> Cursed be the hour and cursed be the day
> on which they gave me over to the school,
> to learn my letters, as though I could live off them!'
>   *Ptochoprodromika* IV.1–22 (ed. 1909): my translation

After the Fourth Crusade of 1204, which left much of the Greek-speaking world under Western control, there followed a greater diversification of genres, including translations and free adaptations from Italian and French models. Vernacular verse from the thirteenth to fifteenth centuries includes romances of chivalry, fabulous tales of Alexander the Great, Apollonios of Tyre and other semi-legendary figures, verse chronicles, animal fables, satirical and moralising verses, historical and religious laments, as well as short but finely-wrought love lyrics. Many of these poems were recast into rhyming couplets—introduced under Western influence from the late fourteenth century—and eventually printed as popular chapbooks at the Greek presses

of Venice. Something of the dramatic change in reading habits effected by the introduction of these chapbooks in rhymed verse can be glimpsed from a Dialogue between Student and Bookseller which prefaces the 1539 edition of the first modern Greek translation of the Homeric poem, the *Battle Between Frogs and Mice*:

> *Bookseller*: The most wise Homer's *Battle of Frogs and Mice*.
> *Student*: That won't do for me; its language is too hard.
> *Bookseller*: No, its language is quite plain; it has been transformed, and from metric verse it has now been put in rhyme.
> *Student*: It's in rhyme? Then give it to me, don't delay!

Such texts enjoyed lasting influence and wide diffusion throughout the period of Ottoman rule, with re-printings at regular intervals from the early sixteenth to the mid-nineteenth centuries. Designed primarily for popular rather than learned consumption, these chapbooks form our earliest corpus of printed literary texts in modern Greek. Even texts which never became chap-books (such as the Ptochoprodromic Poems, the epic romance *Digenes Akrites*, and some of the romances of chivalry), where they survive in more than one manuscript or version can be shown to have been creatively rehandled to absorb oral-traditional material. Nor was it a one-way process: many *paramythia*, those enchanting but undeservedly neglected wondertales of Greek folklore, have absorbed themes, motifs and even formulas from these texts, which were read out on formal and informal occasions by village priests and schoolmasters to literate and illiterate audiences throughout the Ottoman period. Yet other texts — above all the religious laments — seem to have passed directly into oral tradition, with the result that it is still possible to hear in parts of Greece on Good Friday chanted recitations of the Virgin's Lament which bear striking resemblances to versions in manuscripts preserved from the thirteenth century onwards.

For these reasons, the legacy of Byzantine literature is inextricably inter-connected with the formative centuries of modern Greek literature, oral and written. Most texts mentioned so far are anonymously or dubiously transmitted, and of uncertain provenance, due to the absence of dialect features. In areas which remained in Western hands after the collapse of the Byzantine Empire in 1453, such as Crete, Cyprus, Naxos and Rhodes, local dialect rather than archaising Greek had long been customary for legal and administrative purposes. By 1400, poets began to cultivate and refine their local dialects as a medium for a more individualised literary expression — for the first time since classical antiquity. Thanks to these texts, we can conclude that the Cretan and Cypriot dialects, for example, had already acquired their major distinctive features of today. From Rhodes, held by the Knights of Saint John until 1522, come several historical laments, and a corpus of love poems (in traditional fifteen-syllable verse) which combine the delicacy of European courtly love lyrics with the allusive power of the folk tradition. From Cyprus, held by the House of Lusignan from 1191 and then by the Venetians until its capture by the Ottomans in 1571, there survive dialect legal texts (*The Assizes of Cyprus*), prose chronicles and histories such as Leontios Makhairas' *History of the Sweet Island of Cyprus*, and a sixteenth-century manuscript of over 150 love sonnets, translated or freely adapted into local dialect and delicate hendecasyllabic meter from Italian Renaissance prototypes, yet injecting much of the freshness of Cypriot oral traditions. But it was above all on the island of Crete that the Italian Renaissance made its mark: from *circa* 1400 until its capture by the Ottomans from the Venetians in 1669, there flourished a rich tradition of poetry and drama in elevated forms of Cretan dialect, often in a different writing system (the Roman alphabet employed in accordance with the phonological rules of Italian). One of the earliest dialect poems to be printed, published first at Venice in 1509, was Bergadis' *Apokopos*, probably composed around 1400: in a dream descent to the

Underworld, the poet-narrator challenges both religious and traditional views of death and the afterlife, in verses which enchant to this day because of the poet's lyrical insistence that life be celebrated over death. Despite (or because of?) the fact that this, and other poems like it, were condemned as 'satanic verses' in the mid-sixteenth century by the theologian Pachomios Rhousanos in an open letter of protest to the Printers of Venice, they remained widely read and much loved by the Greek people.

The best-known works from the Cretan period date from the last century of Venetian rule, c.1570–1669: three plays by George Chortatsis, his urban comedy *Katzourbos*; his pastoral tragi-comedy *Panoria*; and his tragedy *Erofili*; the anonymously transmitted religious play *Abraham's Sacrifice*; Marc-Antonio Foskolos' urban comedy *Fortounatos*; and the long verse romance by Vitzensos Kornaros, the *Erotokritos*. All works show close interaction with Italian and other Western models; but they are creative rehandlings rather than slavish imitations, imbued with a freshness, spontaneity and questioning humanity which owe much to native popular traditions as well as to the religious tolerance fostered by the diversity of Cretan culture. It is a tribute to the literary taste of ordinary Greeks that many of these works remained popular through chapbooks and live dramatic representations throughout the Ottoman period, at a time when they were despised as vulgar by the intelligentsia and condemned as immoral by the Church. Like the post-Byzantine romances and fables, the stories of 'Neronfili' and 'Rotokritos' fed back into the folk imagination long before they were reclaimed as an integral part of the demotic heritage by later 19th century scholars.

After the fall of Crete to the Ottomans in 1669, many Cretans fled to the Ionian Isles, taking with them their books, manuscripts and oral traditions. It was through the Ionian Isles — never part of the Ottoman Empire — that contact between centers of learning in Italy and the Greek-speaking world was maintained. While not renowned for its literary creativity, the period between 1669 and the War of Independence (1821 –28) saw crucial changes, both in the structure of Greek intellectual life and in Western attitudes to Greece. First, among Greeks: on the one hand, there emerged a new intelligentsia, — usually educated, and often domiciled, abroad — whose scholarly output was printed at new Greek presses at Jassy, Bucharest, Constantinople, Jerusalem and Petrograd. Some were later translated into other languages (Korydalleus' *Logic*, for example, into Romanian and Turkish) and diffused to many parts of the Ottoman Empire. Greek letters thus formed a bridge between East and West. On the other hand, the increasingly apparent influence of the European Enlightenment met with disapproval in more conservative quarters of the Orthodox Church, although it would be a mistake to view the Church's role as negative or negligible, especially as regards popular education. Whereas most educated Greeks at the turn of the eighteenth century despised popular culture for what they saw as manifest signs of Ottoman enslavement, the Church — almost as suspicious of Western ideas as it was inimical to the Infidel — was far less remote from the people, and disseminated basic literacy. Alongside more serious secular and religious works we have a third strand in pre-revolutionary literary productivity: simple prose tales of local saints and heroes, whose legendary deeds had saved their communities from infidel and barbarian attacks and from natural disaster, or who had led their people to new village sites — a veritable blend of popular religion, history and romance. It was partly from the spirit of such humble works as the *Chronicle of Galaxeidi* (1703) or the sermons of Kosmas the Aetolian that the more far-sighted precursors of the War of Independence, like Rhigas Velestinlis and the anonymous author of the *Greek Nomarchy* (1814) drew inspiration for their own writings in an attempt to bridge the gap between ideals for national liberation and rural reality, where fierce local rivalries often proved stronger than abstract notions of Hellenism. These three strands — intellectual, ecclesiastical and popular — interacted in complex ways; but by and large

it was the radical intellectuals who provided the main impetus for progress and change along Western lines; the Orthodox Church which formed the unifying spiritual force throughout the period of Ottoman rule; while popular culture played a more dynamic role than is usually recognised in preserving the memory of old favorites. Comparisons are dangerous; but Greek peasants of the Ottoman period, if no less illiterate, were certainly more in touch with their past literary heritage than their European counterparts, perhaps because their best-loved texts were felt to be an inalienable part of their 'Greekness'. Meanwhile, the geographical fragmentation of the Greek mainland and Aegean islands, the uneven patterns of foreign occupation, and the sheer diversity of cultural influences rendered possible the variegated mosaic of local traditions in music, song, dance, weaving and copperware (to name but a few examples) which remains such a striking feature of Balkan and Anatolian cultures to this day.

Until the rise of modern Western theories of nation, race and the origins of civilisation from the late eighteenth century, the heterogeneity and diversity of Greek culture passed without comment. European travellers and diplomats to Greek lands, from Liutprand of Cremona in the tenth century to Pierre Augustin Guys in the eighteenth century, may have had their stereotypes, both positive and negative; but they never doubted—if they ever thought of it—that present-day Greeks were the descendants of the ancients. However, from around 1770 onwards, new theories were being advanced leading to a radical reversal by the 1840's, culminating in the notorious racism of the Austrian historian Jakob von Fallmerayer, who claimed in his histories of Greece (1830 and 1845) that the Slavic and Albanian incursions during the early middle ages were so overwhelming that not a drop of 'pure' Hellenic blood flowed in modern Greek veins. It is usual for Greeks, and convenient for Western Europeans, to cast Fallmerayer as the only enemy of neohellenism. But, without in any way exonerating Fallmerayer, the truth is more complex, since his theories merely systematise in extreme form the Western romantic idealisation of ancient Greece as it was being redefined by the emergent disciplines of classics and philology. They also coincide precisely with nascent theories of biological racism, which held that miscegenation was directly linked with cultural and moral decay, thereby providing convenient justification for the continued subjugation of the Greeks to the Ottomans just when the Greek nation-state was struggling to establish itself. If ancient Greek civilisation as a miracle of 'pure Hellenism' is a romantic fabrication of the West, then the perennial dilemma of national and cultural identity faced by modern Greeks— 'how closely do we resemble our noble ancient forbears?' 'do we belong to East or West?' 'are we Hellenes or Romioi?'—is revealed as a chimera. Modern Greek culture does not have to claim straight linear descent from antiquity in order to prove its validity; rather, creative interaction and violent coexistence with Balkan and Anatolian peoples have been facts of life since prehistoric times, as the history of the Greek language itself shows.

During the course of the later nineteenth century two inter-connected movements provided the major focus in the search for Greek identity and links with the past, partly in response to Fallmerayer's racism: the folklore movement, which saw the folk traditions as a reflection of the 'eternal spirit of the Greek people'; and the demoticist movement, which emphasised the unbroken linguistic continuity from Homeric Greek to the modern popular language. In fact, interest in Greek folk songs came initially from scholars and poets in Europe at the turn of the eighteenth century, when young and ambitious romantics were beginning to exploit folk poetry, and above all the ballad, for its potential contribution towards new national and personal forms of poetic expression. The first anthologies were made by Swiss, German and French scholars, mainly from materials collected from expatriate Greek informants. Claude Fauriel's *Chants Populaires de la Grèce moderne* (Paris: 1824 and 1826) excited immediate and

favorable attention among literary circles in France, Germany and Russia, but not much in Greece, where the intelligentsia still despised the folk songs as vulgar and contaminated. By contrast, the Greek folklore movement of the 1880's onwards was strongly influenced by survivalist theories which sought above all to demonstrate links with ancient Greece and to minimise or deny the influence of neighboring cultures. Today, there has been an understandable reaction: on the one hand, folklorists have shifted their focus from links with the past to social context and artistic function, regarding the search for continuity as 'outmoded'; on the other hand, there is a discernible tendency among intellectuals to look down on oral traditions and their influence on modern poets and prose-writers as 'naive', 'backward', 'ethnocentric'; instead, they draw attention to writers like Roidis, Cavafy and Karyotakis as more in tune with Western literary tastes. Rather than once more over-reacting to prevailing European trends, the best way to combat the idealisation and appropriation of ancient Greek civilisation, with its inevitable concomitant denigration and marginalisation of modern Greece, is through diachronic studies, both oral and literary, which can avoid the pitfalls of survivalism, Eurocentrism and Hellenocentrism by taking fuller account of East-West interaction and the ethno-linguistic diversity within the Greek-speaking world.

A few examples may illustrate the plurality of Greek literary voices since the early nineteenth century. Two outstanding poets of the revolutionary period were Dionysios Solomos (1798–1857) and Andreas Kalvos (1792–1869), both born on the island of Zakynthos and nurtured in the Italian literary tradition. In contrast to the patriotic rhetoric of Solomos' *Hymn to Liberty* (1823)—the first verses of which now constitute the National Anthem of Greece—his more mature poetry expresses a profound sense of the tragic contradictions inherent in the human condition, composed in finely chiselled demotic verse which draws both on folk song and on Cretan Renaissance literature. His *Free Besieged* 'fails' in Western romantic terms to 'tell the story' of the heroic struggle of the Greeks during the Siege of Messolonghi (1825–26): the three drafts he never completed consist only of poetic fragments of extraordinary lyrical intensity, linked by short narrative passages in limpid prose which owes much to the language of the Greek Church. It is precisely Solomos' 'failure' as a romantic which appeals to readers today. His *Ode on the Destruction of Psara* encapsulates in six dense lines the fragmentation and devastation which accompanied the emergence of the modern Greek nation:

On Psara's blackened ridge
walks Glory, alone,
musing on illustrious young men,
wearing a crown on her hair
made from a few odd weeds
left on the desolate earth.
    Solomos, *Collected Poems* (ed. 1948–60): my translation

Nor can Kalvos be conveniently placed in European literature. Unlike European poets, his 'mother' tongue (Greek) was also his 'other', poetic tongue, his first language being Italian: his entire *oeuvre* consists of only twenty Odes (1824 and 1826), composed in archaising Greek and Italianate verse forms; yet his lyrical imagery, perfection of form and fiery patriotism give his verse a quality neither classical nor romantic, neither surrealist nor modernist, but with elements of each, as Elytis has commented.

The debate between the 'purists' and the 'demoticists' dates from the late eighteenth century in its modern form. At first sight, it appears to be a straightforward question

of language: is demotic or purist (*katharevousa*) the most 'genuine' descendant of ancient Greek, and therefore the most apt medium for literary expression? From the vantage-point of the present (that is, since 1976, when the purist language ceased to be the official language of the state) we can see that both sides have a case; also, that both shared the assumption that the modern language must be coherent and uniform in its relation to the ancient. But by the latter part of the nineteenth century, each side was vying for hegemony of the modern literary canon. As Cavafy once wrily remarked, the demoticists wanted to throw half the Greek language into the river, while the purists wished to throw the other half into the sea. During the 1880's, the 'language question' entered a decisive new phase, just when the folklore movement approached its peak. First, the Paris-trained Greek linguist Jean Psichari published his literary manifesto *My Journey* (1888), in which he argued on the basis of historical linguistics (itself an offshoot of romantic philology) that demotic had evolved organically from ancient Greek, with its own literary pedigree, and that the purist was an artificial construct based on an archaising and imitative tradition dating back to the second century A.D. *My Journey* appeared at a time of upsurge in patriotic interest in the folk traditions, for reasons touched on above. Second, Kostes Palamas (1859– 1943) demonstrated in practice and on a grand scale the power and richness of demotic as a medium for literary expression. Literary hegemony was gradually wrested from the purists, and the time for a revision of the poetic canon was ripe. 'I cannot be merely the poet of myself', Palamas wrote, in the Preface to the *Twelve Lays of the Gipsy* (in conscious opposition to prevailing European literary vogues) . . . 'I am a poet of my age and of my nation' (1907). His long epico-lyric poem gives expression to the force of the unbroken continuity of Hellenism from a new standpoint—that of the Outsider, the quintessentially romantic Gipsy who tries but fails to come to terms with his heterogeneous past. Although now regarded as 'outmoded', some day Palamas will be recognised as the great poet that he was, despite the 'limitations' of his age and nation, as viewed from Western perspectives. The same sense that imbues his work of Poet as 'bard of the nation' has inspired poets ever since, from ideological perspectives as different as Angelos Sikelianos, Kostas Varnalis, Yiannis Ritsos, George Seferis and Odysseas Elytis. It is a keynote which gives priority to voice over text, rendering to modern Greek poetry a song-like quality, whether declamatory, tragic or nostalgic. Although different from that of Western modernist or post-modernist poetry, this voice has significant parallels in other non-Western cultures where the gap between oral and written literature is less wide, and where the poet retains something of his mantic character, as in Africa, Latin America, Turkey, or indeed in ancient Greece.

Greece has enjoyed throughout the advantages of a heterogeneous tradition: almost contemporary with Kostes Palamas was C.P. Cavafy (1863–1933). Born in Alexandria, Cavafy exploits the full range of the Greek linguistic register, eschewing the rhetorical and lyrical modes for the dramatic and ironic, while drawing on the Hellenic past in order to explore its gaps, interstices and discontinuities, giving greater emphasis to the textual than to the oral tradition. Too often regarded as idiosyncratically 'Alexandrian', Cavafy in fact stands in an alternative bibliophile tradition which can be traced back through Emmanuel Roidis and Adamantios Korais to the scholars of Byzantium and of his native Alexandria. Although he founded no school of poetry, his challenge to the demotic canon has been taken up by Kostas Karyotakis, Kostas Kavadias, Andreas Embirikos and others, including women, whose 'different voice' has gone largely unacknowledged, whether sung, as in the folk laments—which have inspired so many modern male poets, musicians and singers— or more private, as in the poetry of Zoe Karelli, Katerina Angelaki-Rooke, Maria Laina, Olga Broumas and the prose of Elisabeth Mountza-Martinengou, Melpo Axioti and Maro Douka.

Greek prose fiction has attracted much less critical attention than poetry.
Paradoxically at first sight, prose was slower than poetry to adopt demotic, possibly
due to the absence of consistent models which had existed in poetry since the twelfth
century. The best-known prose works of the nineteenth century are either non-fictional,
like the *Memoirs* of General Makryiannis, or written in registers ranging from the
'high' puristic Greek of Emmanuel Roidis' *Pope Joan* (1866) to the 'mixed' language
of the short stories of George Vizyenos (1849–96) and Alexandros Papadiamandis
(1851–1911), both of whom draw on various registers to convey different narrative
tones. During the twentieth century, demotic has prevailed as the standard medium,
with considerable literary use of local dialect (Stratis Myrivilis, Pandelis Prevelakis,
Nikos Kazantzakis). But the differences between Western European and Greek fiction
remain: Greek prose fiction refuses to conform to Western norms of the classic realist
novel of the nineteenth century. Notably absent in Greek fiction is the theme of
romantic love leading to marriage, as the (implied) 'happy ending', as is the theme of
marital bliss. Love is tinged with violence, even death (Andreas Karkavitsas,
Konstantinos Theotokis, Gregorios Xenopoulos, Nikos Kazantzakis); often illicit, it
comes into conflict with traditional values, according to which marriage is a matter of
duty and convenience; hence the focal areas of conflict tend to be intra-familial, as in
the folk ballads. Moreover, twentieth-century Greek inter-war and post-war
experiences have impinged so deeply on the nation's consciousness that Greek prose
fiction, whether urban or rural in setting, *avant-garde* or traditional in conception, has
tended to focus attention on the individual (usually male) within the context of war,
upheaval and rapid change. Finally, myth, fantasy and violence are allowed a special
space, not least because of the ongoing but hitherto largely unresearched influence of
the Greek *paramythia*, oral wondertales which are closer to the East than the West.
Prose writers, no less than poets, have drawn consciously and unconsciously from the
classical past for themes, imagery, motifs and names, from Stratis Myrivilis and
George Theotokas in the 1930's to Kostas Tachtsis and Margarita Karapanou in the
1960's. This is neither escapism nor nostalgia, but creative exploitation of past
traditions. It has significant parallels in recent widely acclaimed Latin-American and
Afro-American novels, such as those of Gabriel Garcia Marquez, Alice Walker, and
Toni Morrison. Their success should encourage others to follow Olga Broumas and
Irini Spanidou in making Greek women's voices heard in American literature.

The distinctive—if sometimes conflicting—qualities of modern Greek literature
may be summarised as follows. First, Greek folk traditions, of a richness and diversity
unmatched in Europe, have fed both from and into literary composition in a variety of
ways at least since the twelfth century, and will continue to do so for the foreseeable
future: the poet can still speak—or sing—in a public voice, in accordance with the
ancient meanings of *ode* and *melos*. Second, alongside the folk culture and interacting
with it, there has existed the tempering influence of a prestigious and coherent learned
tradition, whose terms of reference—again unlike any Western European literature—
can be traced back to late antiquity. Third, there is the religious tradition, which, like
the literary one, includes popular lore and practice as well as official forms. These
three strands, and discordant elements within them, have often conflicted and
attempted to efface each other, especially since Eurocentric notions preferring either
Voice over Word or Writing over Speech have prevailed from Rousseau to Derrida.
But in Greece, interpenetration has, in practice, been continuous. As with the
Prodromic Poems, the Cypriot love sonnets, and the poetry and drama of Renaissance
Crete, so today all traditions can and should be included under 'modern Greek', and
exploited in ways relevant to our age. In Western terms, it is as if medieval and
Renaissance Latin had remained a living part of modern culture. So far as 'foreign'
influences are concerned, the debt of Cretan literature to Italy, or of Greek poetry and
prose—from the Enlightenment to Modernism—to Western Europe, or of Greek

folklore to neighboring cultures, is undeniable; but in each case it has proved an enriching interaction. Greece may have been a pawn in the political games played between the great powers of East and West: culturally, she can hold her own. The classical heritage has remained a source of inspiration, not just a reminder of the 'glory that was Greece', as the European Philhellenes of the nineteenth century would have us believe, but a constant challenge to Greeks everywhere to reappropriate Hellenism from the Mandarins of the West.

A poem by Cavafy (circulated in 1917) epitomises the diversity of Greek letters, expressing poignantly the urgency that the past and the 'other' be included in the present. The speaker is an Alexandrian of the early seventh century A.D. — just before the Arab conquest — who asks another Alexandrian, Raphael — an Egyptian — to compose an epitaph in perfect Greek for their mutual friend, Ammonis (another Egyptian, whose name suggests the god Amon, 'the hidden one'), a Greek poet who has died at the young age of 29. It must do justice to his physical beauty as well as to his exquisite Greek. What Cavafy is saying, here and elsewhere, is that Greece has already been plural in literary, linguistic, religious traditions — and ethnic ones too!

> *For Ammonis, who died at 29 years in 610*
> Raphael, a few verses they ask of you
> as epitaph for the poet Ammonis to compose.
> Something very finely felt and polished. You will do it,
> you are the one qualified to write as befits
> the poet Ammonis, our own.
>
> Of course you will speak of his poems —
> but speak also of his beauty,
> of his subtle beauty we loved.
> Your Greek is always fine and musical.
> But we want all your craft now.
> Our sorrow and love penetrate a foreign language.
> Into the foreign language pour your Egyptian feeling.
>
> Raphael, let your verses be so written
> as to contain — you know — our life within them,
> so rhythm and every phrase might show
> an Alexandrian writing of an Alexandrian.
>> *Poems* (ed. 1963): my translation

ii.   *The Harvard collection of modern Greek books and manuscripts**

The Harvard College Library houses today one of the richest collections of modern Greek books outside of Greece, comprising over 80,000 volumes. Among them are rare books and manuscripts (of which the present exhibition represents only a selection), first editions of folklore collections, modern authors and Western travellers, as well as an unusually complete set of nineteenth-century periodicals and historical documents. The story of its acquisition provides a fascinating insight into the history of modern Greek scholarship in the West and its interaction with Western philhellenism and with Greeks from Greece and the diaspora. It also tells us that great library collections do not happen of their own accord, but have always depended on the devotion and generosity of scholars and patrons of all kinds. Three major stages may be traced: first, random acquisitions by early American philhellenes and Greek bibliophiles (up to *circa* 1840); second, systematic collecting both by Harvard

hellenists and by the College itself (up to 1900); and third, the expansion and consolidation of the collection during the present century thanks to an extremely fortunate collaboration of Harvard scholars and librarians with friends of Greece, including many from the Greek-American community of the greater Boston area.

The first to mention modern Greek holdings in the Boston area was the classical scholar — and probably the earliest American philhellene — Edward Everett (1794–1865), who recorded in 1863 'some ten books in the Romeic [= modern Greek]'. Everett fixed the pattern for future scholars when he set out in 1819 for Italy, Greece and Turkey, making the acquaintance *en route* in Paris of the eminent Greek scholar Adamantios Korais, who furnished him with letters of introduction to the 'elite of modern Greece'. He purchased for Harvard in Constantinople six early manuscripts, the first ones in modern Greek to be brought to America. Today, Korais' letters to Everett are to be found in the library of the Massachusetts Historical Society, while Harvard holds important editions of all Korais' major works, many editions of his correspondence, and a large number of his single works. Everett's example was followed by another American philhellene, Samuel Gridley Howe (M.D. Harvard, 1824), who visited Greece in 1825 and whose involvement with the War of Independence and the later Cretan struggles for liberation is recorded in his journals, correspondence, and other papers, all to be found in Harvard libraries. Probably the first actually to teach modern Greek at Harvard was Colonel Alexander Negris, veteran of the War of Independence, who arrived in Boston late in 1827: College Records of 15 September 1828 include the entry 'Any students who wish may be permitted to attend the Instruction of Mr. Negris in the Modern Greek, *at such times as not to interfere with their regular exercises*' (emphases mine). In the same year he published his *Grammar of the Modern Greek Language* (Boston, 1828), the first to be printed in the U.S.; yet he failed to make an adequate living. In May 1829 he moved to Providence, Rhode Island, and thence in July to Europe, where he finally settled in Edinburgh to continue his teaching and editing activities.

Undoubtedly the major stimulus for the development of modern Greek studies at Harvard was provided by the two key figures, Cornelius Conway Felton (1807–1862) and Evangelos Apostolides Sophokles (c. 1807–1883). Felton, Eliot Professor of Greek from 1834 and President of the College from 1860, had an enduring interest in modern Greek life, letters and education, as well as in the Classics, together with a perception of the value of interconnecting the two which antedates developments in Europe. His publications on modern Greek topics include *Select Modern Greek Poems* (Cambridge, 1838), *Selections from Modern Greek Writers in Prose and Poetry* (Cambridge, 1855), *Schools of Modern Greece* (1861), and a posthumous collection of lectures entitled *Greece: Ancient and Modern* (Boston, 1866). These anthologies show a perspicacious appreciation of the contemporary relevance of Greek writers, including extracts from Konstantinos Paparrigopoulos' *History of Greece* (1853), from Spyridon Trikoupis' *History of the Greek Revolution* (1853–7), from Alexander Soutsos, Rigas Velestinlis, Athanasios Christopoulos, as well as examples from heroic and other folk ballads. In addition to his generous gifts of books to the Library made throughout his lifetime, Felton's considerable personal library was donated by his heirs in two major stages: 160 items in 1868, and no fewer than 1,704 items in 1885, including volumes sent to him by Greek scholars with whom he had kept in contact throughout his career.

It was Felton who was responsible for the first official appointment in modern Greek studies at Harvard. Sophokles had arrived in Boston in July 1828, on the invitation of the American Board of Commissioners for Foreign Missions. Educated in Cairo under the tutelage of his paternal uncle, the monk Konstantinos Sinaitis (whose books he inherited and in whose memory the Constantius Memorial Fund was set up at the Harvard College Library in 1883), and later at the famous school of Miliai on Mount

Pelion, Sophokles came to the U.S. with an impeccable knowledge of Arabic and Hebrew, in addition to his command of ancient and modern Greek and of the major European languages. After a brief period at Yale as private tutor (1836) and as official Instructor (1837–40), where he published the first demotic grammar to be printed on American soil (*A Romeic Grammar*: Hartford, 1842), Sophokles was named Teacher of Greek at Harvard in 1842, a position which led to what was probably the first tenured appointment in Modern Greek in the Western world. His eventual appointment as Professor of ancient, medieval and modern Greek was the first of its kind, and at a time when it mattered most for Greece (1860–83). Like Felton, he donated to the Library throughout his lifetime numerous rare books and manuscripts: his final bequest (1887) lists 211 volumes, 129 pamphlets and seven newspapers, including rare items from the presses of Venice and Vienna. On Felton's death in 1862, he wrote a funerary epigram in elegiac couplets as a tribute to his friend and mentor.

The earliest evidence for large-scale purchasing of modern Greek books by Harvard College dates from June 1855, when the Library acquired the works of prominent intellectuals and writers, such as Spyridon Zambelios, Dimitrios Vernardakis, Alexandros and Panayiotis Soutsos, I.A. Neroulos; as well as the priceless first edition of the Provisional Constitution of Greece (Corinth, 1822), purchased for the princely sum of one drachma. Throughout the rest of the nineteenth century, and the whole of the twentieth, it has remained standard practice to purchase modern Greek books on a regular basis. To the already impressive collection was added in 1899–1900 an important collection of works on the Crusades and the Latin East (the Riant Library), purchased for Harvard by Professor A.C. Coolidge and his father, J.Randolph Coolidge: 870 volumes, in addition to 100 manuscripts and 99 *incunabula*, found a home in the Ottoman and modern Greek sections of the Library.

The next Greek scholar of importance, trained in the Classics at Harvard (A.B. *summa cum laude* 1911, Ph.D. 1915), was Aristides Phoutrides (1887–1923). Initially a supporter of puristic Greek, his acquaintance with the poet Kostes Palamas led him to an appreciation of demotic Greek literature, and to the publication of important critical works and translations for the first time in the U.S. After his death, part of his personal library was donated by his widow, Margaret Garrison Phoutrides, who also endowed a scholarship in her husband's memory. Another major accession was offered in 1943 by the American Board of Commissioners for Foreign Missions, which deposited in Harvard Library a substantial collection of papers, tracts and books dealing with foreign missions to Greece and Turkey between 1820 and 1869. The collection, which contains items printed at the Mission's own presses in Malta and Smyrna, includes the only known surviving copy of the first edition of the highly successful and widely disseminated Greek translation of Leigh Richmond's Protestant tract, *The Dairyman's Daughter* (Malta, 1822). It is from documents of this kind that the social historian can reconstruct the state of religion and education in the daily life of ordinary Greeks of the time, as well as the activities of foreign missions.

In all the major areas of Greek bibliography, Harvard holdings are outstanding: history; folklore; linguistics; and literature from the medieval period to the present day. The history collection, which is particularly rich in documents relating to the *Philike Hetairia*, the War of Independence and early constitutional history, provides an excellent illustration of how Harvard library policy has continued to strengthen the value of nineteenth-century holdings: as recently as 1966, the Library purchased from a private collection an additional 160 items on the Greek Revolution; while in the summer of 1987, Houghton Library's indefatigable Curator of Rare Books, Mr. Stoddard, discovered in Paris a unique and complete set of minutes taken at meetings in Paris of European philhellenes, held between the years 1815 and 1833. Subsequently, funds contributed by Friends of the College Library have made possible the purchase of these documents. Similarly, the folklore collection has continued to

expand, above all with the acquisition (1965–72) of the first known systematic collection of Greek Shadow Theater (Karaghiozes), comprising seventy tape recordings (most from live performances) by nineteen of the best puppeteers from the regions of Athens and the northern Peloponnese, eighteen tapes of professional life histories, 24 actual shadow puppets, and numerous documents, films, slides and photographs. This unique and fascinating collection of oral theater was made possible by the initiative of Mr. Mario Rinvolucri and Professor Cedric Whitman, and by funding from the National Endowment for the Humanities. As for modern poetry, the generosity of Professor George Savidis, first incumbent of the George Seferis Chair of Modern Greek Studies (1977–85), has enriched the Library with a number of manuscripts, notes and rare first editions from the works of C.P. Cavafy and George Seferis.

Last but not least, mention should be made of two of the most important bequests of funds for the purchase of modern Greek books and for the promotion of modern Greek studies, without which the collection could not have continued to grow: the Raphael Demos Fund (1964); and above all, the Harry Knowles Messenger and Ada Messenger Fund (1968). The generosity of these and other benefactors has hitherto ensured the continuous growth of the Harvard Collection, as well as the indelibility of their own role in its formation.

iii. *Modern Greek studies at Harvard*

As George Savidis pointed out with such eloquence on the occasion of the second annual Nicholas Christopher Memorial Lecture (December 4, 1987), which opened the exhibition on which the present Catalogue is based, fine collections of books are true 'anthologies', as choice and beautiful as flowers. Like flowers, books need to be cultivated; and that means *used* by present and future generations of scholars. As we have seen, the seeds for the growth of modern Greek studies at Harvard were sown at the beginning of the last century, to be fostered by scholars with a classical training such as Felton and Sophokles. From later in the nineteenth century until the present day, the philological tradition has combined with pioneering studies and collections in oral literature by such outstanding Harvard scholars as F.J. Child, G.L. Kittredge, Cedric Whitman, Milman Parry and Albert B. Lord, with the result that the study of folklore and mythology at Harvard now covers — among others — the Anglo-Saxon, Celtic, Scandinavian, Balkan and Anatolian cultural areas. The classical connections held by at least three of these scholars make it eminently appropriate that the George Seferis Chair of Modern Greek Studies at Harvard, established in 1977 and funded by Greek monies, should have been situated in the Department of the Classics, where both oral and literary strands of modern Greek can be studied in conjunction with Byzantine literature and history, and with the ancient past. Collaboration with scholars in related fields, such as Comparative Literature, History and Anthropology, is welcomed.

The first incumbent of the Seferis Chair, George Savidis, initiated a program of undergraduate and graduate courses admirably suited to the requirements of students from a wide range of literary and linguistic disciplines. It is thanks to his meticulous scholarship and archival research that editions of so many modern Greek authors are now widely available. Savidis also laid solid foundations for the study of modern Greek as one of the three components for the degree of Ph.D. in Comparative Literature.

Now that the Chair has been established on a full-time basis, the major tasks are: first and foremost, to develop the newly approved Ph.D. program of modern Greek within the Department of the Classics (our first graduate enrolled in 1988 to study Greek shadow theater), and to expand the numbers of doctoral candidates studying modern Greek in the Departments of Comparative Literature (currently 5), Romance

Linguistics (1) and Anthropology (1). Second, at the undergraduate level, modern Greek courses can be made relevant and attractive to majors and concentrators in other fields, such as the Classics, Folklore and Mythology, Women's Studies, Religion, Anthropology, History, as well as to students in the Core Curriculum and in Harvard Extension School. The Harvard program in modern Greek offers many advantages: training is provided across a wide range of linguistic, philological, literary, historical and anthropological skills in order to equip students to take full advantage of the rich primary source material. Areas which remain to be developed—and where library holdings can be expected to expand—include early vernacular verse and prose, and above all the poetry and drama of Renaissance Crete. Already in possession of some rare printed editions of Cretan texts (including the 1681 edition of Bounialis' poem, *The War of Crete*), Harvard needs to extend its collection of manuscripts and printed texts so as to tell a fuller story of the transmission and reception of Cretan and other vernacular literatures during the seventeenth and eighteenth centuries. Towards a deeper appreciation of the diversity of popular culture at this formative stage of modern Greek consciousness, it is also to be hoped that the rich resources in Ottoman and other Balkan studies can be fully co-ordinated with those of modern Greek. It is only through the active collaboration of scholars in all these disciplines that the relevance and value of modern Greek—hitherto marginalised somewhere between East and West, the Classics and the Orient—can be recognised and appreciated. Harvard has the resources, and the friends, for this to become a reality.

Margaret Alexiou
George Seferis Professor of Modern Greek Studies
Harvard University   *May, 1989*

*This summary is based on the excellent article entitled "The Modern Greek Collection in the Harvard College Library," *Harvard Library Bulletin* 19 (1971), 221–43, by Evro Layton.

Liturgical Books

Because of the capture of Byzantium by the Turks in 1453, the Greeks did not benefit immediately from the invention of the art of printing. Many of the Greek intellectuals sought refuge in the West, especially in Italy and particularly at Venice, where they helped to spread knowledge and appreciation of the Greek classical authors. It was not until the end of the fifteenth century, however, that at least two books were printed with Greek readers and not the West in mind. Both were Psalters printed in Venice. During the first decades of the sixteenth century more liturgical books were printed in Venice for the use of an ever increasing Greek community and for export to the eastern Mediterranean. In 1509 Zacharias Kalliergis of Crete, the most famous Greek printer of the Renaissance, issued the first edition of the *Horologion* and in 1520, after he moved to Rome, he printed the first edition of the *Oktoechos*. The *Psalterion*, the *Oktoechos*, and the *Horologion* were also used as schoolbooks during the years of the Turkish Occupation (1453–1821).

It was not until 1521 that printing for Greek consumption was launched in a more systematic way with the establishment of a publishing firm in Venice which specialized in the production of Greek books for Greek readers. The man behind this project was Andreas Kounadis of Patras, a wealthy businessman residing in Venice who conceived the idea. The firm of Andreas Kounadis and Damiano di Santa Maria — his father-in-law and partner — produced a great number of Greek books during its operations, which lasted until 1553. It published many of the first editions and many reissues of all the liturgical books. Soon after, other printers and publishers, both Italian and Greek began to print liturgical works in Venice. The Greek presses of Venice continued to supply Greek books for Greek readers until the beginning of the twentieth century. It was not until the eighteenth century that presses in other parts of the world with large Greek communities published a small number of liturgical books.

1. Παρακλητική.   MS. on paper   15th century.

This recently acquired manuscript contains the *stichera* and *odes* of the Παρακλητική, known also as the Μεγάλη Ὀκτώηχος, one of the most important liturgical books of the Orthodox Church. It contains all the material found in the Ὀκτώηχος plus the Proper of Vespers, Matins, Lauds and the Mass for each day of the year. It is divided into eight parts, each containing the Office of the week which is sung in one of the eight ecclesiastical modes (ἦχοι). The arrangement of the hymns in the Παρακλητική is attributed to Saint John the Hymnographer.

The manuscript is copied by two different hands of the fifteenth century. The scribes have not yet been identified. The elaborate headpieces found at the beginning of each section and the red decorative initials derive from the late Byzantine tradition. The drawings found in the margins are of later, Western origin.

1986–Harry Knowles Messenger and Ada Messenger Fund

Ἰοῦστινος ὁ Δεκάδυος, τοῖς ἐν Ἑλλάδι γραικοῖς, εὖ πράττειν.

Ἄλλοι μὲν ἄγαν τῶν παρ' Ἕλλησι σοφῶν τε καὶ διδασκάλων συγγράμματα διαφόρους πραγματείας ἐμπεριέχοντα, εἰς κοινὴν τοῖς φιλομαθέσιν ὠφέλειαν ἐν τυπώσει ἐσπουδάκασιν. ἐγὼ δὲ ὑπέρεστι μὲν τῶν, τοῖς δὲ εὐσεβείας ἐρασταῖς κεχαρισμένα πράξειν οἰόμενος, ἐν ὧν πολλάκις ἐν χρείᾳ καθίστανται, τούτων αὐτοὺς εὐπορεῖν προνοήσομαι, εἰς πληθυσμὸν ὅση δύναμις τὴν σπάνιν τῶν θείων γραφῶν, μετακαλεῖν. διὰ φροντίδος πεποίημαι, συνεργῷ τῶν τοιούτων ἐφευρετῇ τε σοφῷ καὶ καθηγεμόνι χρησάμενος. ὅς, ἵνα καὶ αὐτοὶ μὴ ἀγνοῆτε τὸν ἄνδρα, τοῖς γὰρ ἐν Ἰταλίᾳ διαβόητος πᾶσι καθέστηκεν, Ἄλδος τοὐπίκλην Μανούτιος ἐκ τῆς παλαιᾶς Ῥώμης ἕλκων τὸ γένος. ἀνὴρ βίῳ τε καὶ λόγῳ κεκοσμημένος. οὗτος, ἀρετῆς ζήλῳ ἅμα τῇ πρὸς τὰ ἡμέτερα κηδεμονίᾳ τε καὶ στοργῇ, τὴν τῶν γραμμάτων τούτων εὐαρμοστίαν καὶ σύνθεσιν, τῇ τοῦ οἰκείου νοὸς ἐφεῦρεν ὀξύτητι. ἔστι γὰρ βλέπειν τὸν χαρακτῆρα, οὗπερ οὐκ ἄν τις τῶν ἐπὶ τὸ καλλιγραφεῖν χειρισόφων, ἐχάραξεν ὡραιότερον. τούτῳ τοιγαροῦν περὶ τούτων κοινολογούμενος, οὐ μόνον ξυναιροῦντα καὶ προστεταμένον, ἀλλ' ἤδη καὶ αὐτὸν οἴκοθεν ὡρμημένον εὗρον εἰς ταῦτα, καὶ τὴν ἐμὴν ἐπὶ πλέον χρησταῖς ἀγγελίαις ὁρμὴν ἐπιτείνοντα. τὴν γὰρ Μωσέος πεντάτευχον, σὺν τῇ τῆς παλαιᾶς διαθήκης πάσῃ λοιπῇ πραγματείᾳ, ἑβραϊστί. ἑλληνιστί. ῥωμαϊστί, οὐκ εἰς μακρὰν ἐκδώσειν εὐηγγελίσατο σὺν θεῷ. ὧν ἀκούσας αὐτὸς μὲν ὥσπερ ἐν θοίνῃ ὑφ' ἡδονῆς ἐγεγόνειν, εἴτε ἅμα τὰ ἡμέτερα πεπαλαιωμένα τῷ χρόνῳ καὶ ταῖς τῶν πραγμάτων ἀνωμαλίαις ἤδη τυγχάνοντα, νῦν ὡς ἀετοῦ νεότης ἀνακαινίζεσθαι μέλλουσιν. ἐκεῖνον δὲ τοῦ τε τῶν καλῶν ἔρωτος καὶ τῆς χρηστῆς προαιρέσεως ἐμακάρισα. οὐ γὰρ χρημάτων ἐπιθυμία. ἀνώτερον γὰρ ἀνελευθερίας ἁπάσης ἴσμεν οἱ πεπειραμένοι τὸν ἄνδρα. θείῳ δὲ μᾶλλον ζήλῳ πρὸς ταῦτα κεκίνηται. τοῦτον τοίνυν συνεργὸν εὑρηκὼς πρὸς τὰ κάλλιστα, ἔδοξέ μοι τὴν θεόπνευστον βίβλον τῶν θείων πρῶτον ἐντυπῶσαι ψαλμῶν. τὸν ἀρίστως ταύτην καὶ ἀξίως τοῦ ἐν αὐτῷ συνθέμενον πνεύματος προφήτην ἅμα καὶ βασιλέα. ὥσπερ τινὰ πρόδρομον καὶ κήρυκα διαπρύσιον τῶν μετ' οὐ πολὺ τυπωθησομένων ἡμῖν θείων προεκπέμψαι γραφῶν. οὐκ εἰκῇ· μακρὰν γὰρ καὶ τὸ [illegible] ὃ καλεῖν ἡμῖν ἔθος πεντηκοστάριον. μεθ' ὃ τὴν παρακλητικήν, θεοῦ συναιρομένου τυπώσομεν. ταύτῃ γὰρ οὐκ οἶδ' ὅ τι ταῖς κατὰ τόπον ἁπάσαις τοῦ θεοῦ ἐκκλησίαις. πολλήν τε καὶ μεγάλην τὴν χρείαν παρέχεται κατ' ἐξαίρετον δὲ ἡ θεία τῶν ψαλμῶν αὕτη βίβλος. περὶ ἧς φησὶν ὁ θεῖος Χρυσόστομος. μᾶλλον συμφέρειν τῷ κόσμῳ σβεσθῆναι τὸν ἥλιον. ἢ παρὰ τῇ ἐκκλησίᾳ ταύτην ὁσημέραι μὴ ψάλλεσθαι. ὁ δὲ τῆς μέγας αὖθις Βασίλειος. κοινὸν ταμιεῖον ἁπάντων καλῶν αὐτὴν ἀποφαίνεται ὡς τὸ ἐκ πάντων παρεχομένην τοῖς μετὰ προσοχῆς μετερχομένοις ὠφέλιμον τὸ ἑκάστῳ πρόσφορον κατὰ τὴν ἐπιμέλειαν ἐξευρίσκουσαν καθώς, ἐκεῖνος διέξεισιν, ἐν ταῖς εἰς αὐτὴν πλατύτερον ἐξηγήσεσι

α ii

προσκεῖται τοίνυν τὸ κοινωφελὲς τοῦτο τοῖς βουλομένοις ψαλτήριον. ὑμεῖς δὲ ἀνὰ χεῖρας λαβόντες ὅσοι τὰς ψυχὰς εὐρυθμότεροι, καὶ τὴν ἐξ αὐτοῦ ὠφέλειαν καρπωσάμενοι, τὴν τῶν εὐχῶν χορηγίαν ἀντίδοτε, Ἄλδῳ μὲν τῷ φιλέλληνι, ὡς δεξιότητι φύσεως ἐφευρετῇ τοῦ τῶν γραμμάτων γεγενημένῳ χαρακτῆρος (ὡς εἴρηται.) ἐμοὶ δὲ ὡς οὕτω θερμῶς προθυμησαμένῳ τετυπωθῆναι, καὶ μηδενὸς ἀμελήσαντι, τῶν συντελούντων πρὸς τὴν ὀρθότητα. ὑγιέστατα γὰρ ἐντετύπωται καὶ ὀρθότατα.

ἔρρωσθε.

Ψαλμὸς τῷ Δαυὶδ ἀνεπίγραφος παρ' Ἑβραίοις.

ΔΑΔ ΠΡΟΦΗΤΟΥ ΚΑΙ ΒΑΣΙΛΕΩΣ ΜΕΛΟΣ. α΄

ΜΑΚΑΡΙΟΣ Ἀνὴρ ὃς οὐκ ἐπορεύθη ἐν βουλῇ ἀσεβῶν. καὶ ἐν ὁδῷ ἁμαρτωλῶν οὐκ ἔστη. καὶ ἐπὶ καθέδρᾳ λοιμῶν οὐκ ἐκάθισεν. Ἀλλ' ἢ ἐν τῷ νόμῳ κυρίου τὸ θέλημα αὐτοῦ. καὶ ἐν τῷ νόμῳ αὐτοῦ μελετήσει ἡμέρας καὶ νυκτός. Καὶ ἔσται ὡς τὸ ξύλον τὸ πεφυτευμένον παρὰ τὰς διεξόδους τῶν ὑδάτων. ὃ τὸν καρπὸν αὐτοῦ δώσει ἐν καιρῷ αὐτοῦ. Καὶ τὸ φύλλον αὐτοῦ οὐκ ἀπορρυήσεται. καὶ πάντα ὅσα ἂν ποιῇ κατευοδωθήσεται. Οὐχ οὕτως οἱ ἀσεβεῖς οὐχ οὕτως. ἀλλ' ἢ ὡσεὶ χνοῦς ὃν ἐκρίπτει ὁ ἄνεμος ἀπὸ προσώπου τῆς γῆς. Διὰ τοῦτο οὐκ ἀναστήσονται ἀσεβεῖς ἐν κρίσει. οὐδὲ ἁμαρτωλοὶ ἐν βουλῇ δικαίων. Ὅτι γινώσκει κύριος ὁδὸν δικαίων. καὶ ὁδὸς ἀσεβῶν ἀπολεῖται.

α iii

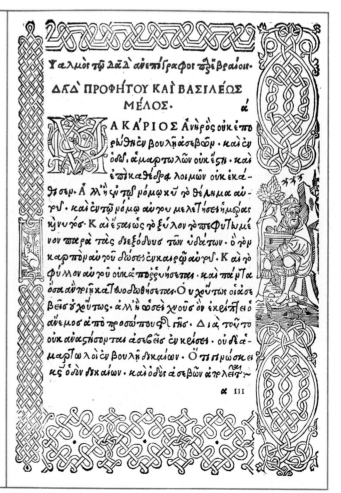

2. Ψαλτήριον. Venetiis, Aldus Manutius Romanus   c. 1496–1498.

This is the only book to come out of the presses of Aldus Manutius which had a Greek clientèle in mind. It was edited by Ioustinos Dekadios of Corfu, who in the preface addressed the Greeks of Greece (*Τοῖς ἔν῀ Ελλάδι Γραικοῖς*) where he mentions that Aldus planned to publish a series of Greek liturgical works for their use. However, none of these were printed, at least by Aldus. The *Ψαλτήριον* was the second Greek book to be printed for liturgical use, the other being also a Psalter printed in 1486 by Alexandros Georgiou of Crete. An earlier Greek-Latin Psalter printed in Milan in 1481 was clearly not printed with a Greek clientèle in mind. It was not until the 1520's that a new era began with the publication of a series of liturgical books.

As is well known to those familiar with the great publishing career of Aldus Manutius, Ioustinos Dekadios was not the only Greek editor to be employed at the Aldine press. Markos Mousouros of Crete (c. 1470–1517) was Aldus' chief collaborator in the editions of Greek classical texts and Ioannes Gregoropoulos, also from Crete was an important member of the Aldine press and a member of the Aldine Academy. Others who also worked for Aldus as editors were Arsenios Apostolis (c. 1469–1535) and Demetrios Doukas (fl. 1508–1527) both also from Crete.

Our knowledge about Ioustinos Dekadios (c. 1472– after 1533) is scant. He went to Venice from his native Corfu when still a young man. In Corfu he was a pupil of Ioannes Moschos, who also taught some Italian humanists, among them Giovanni Bembo. Dekadios was considered one of the best educated Greeks of his generation. Most of our knowledge about his activities is gleaned from his correspondence, much of which unfortunately is not dated. It appears that Ioustinos Dekadios returned to Corfu and taught alongside his former teacher Ioannes Moschos. However, his correspondence indicates that he had kept up with many of the Italian humanists he came to know during his stay in Venice.

1954 – The gift of Mr. and Mrs. Ward M. Canaday.

3. Αἱ Θεῖαι Λειτουργεῖαι.   Ἐν Ῥώμῃ, δεξιότητι Δημητρίου Δουκᾶ τοῦ Κρητός 1526.

This first edition of the liturgies of Saint John Chrysostom, Saint Basil the Great, and the liturgy of the Presanctified was edited and printed by Demetrios Doukas of Crete (fl. 1508–1527). Doukas came to Venice from his native Candia, the present Herakleion, sometime after 1500. His name appears for the first time in one of the Aldine editions, a collection of treatises on rhetoric (*Rhetores in hoc volumine habentur*) dated November 1508–May 1509. Doukas also edited a second work for Aldus, *Plutarchi opuscula*, printed March 1509. Because of his experience as an editor for the Aldine press and his knowledge of Greek Doukas was invited by Cardinal Francisco Jiménez of Spain to take part as an editor of the cardinal's great project, the publishing of the Complutensian Polyglot Bible.

There is information that Doukas was in Spain in 1513 and he probably arrived even earlier. While he worked on the Greek sections of the edition of the Complutensian Bible, he also occupied the chair of Greek from 1513–1518 at the newly established University of Alcalà. By his own account when he arrived in Spain there were no Greek books available for his teaching and despite the fact that he was very busy he was forced to edit, correct, and publish at his own expense two books so that he could use them in his teaching. One of the books was a collection of grammatical works, the second was the poem of Mousaios, *Τὰ κατ' Ἡρὼ καὶ Λέανδρον*, a work which was widely used as a reader during the Renaissance. Both works were published in Alcalá in 1514 by Armao Guillén de Brocar.

After the completion of his editorial duties in late 1517 Doukas must have left Alcalá. We next find him in Rome where he published this first edition of the liturgies. In the preface Doukas addresses himself to orthodox Christians everywhere. The work came out in two issues, the first without the October 28 privilege of Pope Clement VII. Doukas must have also been responsible for the decorations (the headpieces and initials) in the book, which bear a resemblance to those of Zacharias Kalliergis that had been based on

Byzantine models. While in Rome Doukas also taught Greek as a "publicus professor" at the University. The last mention of Demetrios Doukas in the sources is in 1527. It is possible that he had to leave Rome along with many humanists when the city was sacked in May 1527 by the armies of Charles V or he may have perished there.

1954–The gift of Mr. and Mrs. Ward M. Canaday.

4. Στιχηρά ψαλλόμενα μηνὶ Ἰουλίῳ . . . Ἐτυπώθη ἐνετίησι, παρά βαρθολομαίῳ τῷ ἰαννίνῳ ἀναλώμασι καὶ ἐπιμελείᾳ ἀνδρέου τοῦ σπινέλλου 1548.

This *Μηναῖον* for the month of July is one of twelve *Μηναῖα* put out by Andrea Spinelli, a Venetian publisher of Greek liturgical books. The *Μηναῖα* are a set of books, one for each month of the ecclesiastical year, which begins on September 1. Each comprises the Offices commemorating the Proper of the saints. They also contain the lives of the saints and the special hymns and prayers associated with them.

Although the first set of *Μηναῖα* were published between 1526 and 1536, no edition of the *Μηναῖον* of July has survived from that set. The Andrea Spinelli set was the second set to appear in print. It seems that a member of the Venetian Senate who had spent a number of years in Crete, Geronimo Cornelio, had persuaded Spinelli to publish the *Μηναῖα*. This is stated in the dedicatory epistle of Antonios Eparchos to Dionysios II, Patriarch of Constantinople, at the beginning of the *Μηναῖα*. Spinelli engaged the services of a learned Greek cleric then residing in Venice, Nikolaos Malaxos, who later in 1552 was

☙ ΜΗΝ ΙΟΥΛΙΟС ☙

Ἔχων ἡμέρας λα΄ ἡ ἡμέρα ἔχει ὥρας ιδ΄,
καὶ ἡ νὺξ ὥρας ι· εἰς τὴν α΄ τῶν ἁγίων καὶ
θαυματουργῶν ἀναργύρων Κοσμᾶ καὶ
Δαμιανοῦ τῶν ἐν Ῥώμη μαρτυρησάντων·
εἰς τὸ κέ ἐκέκραξα ἱστῶμεν ἃ ϛ΄· & ψάλλο-
μεν στιχηρὰ προσόμοια τῶν ἁγίων γ΄ δεύ-
τερῶντας αὐτά. ἦχ΄ πλ β΄ :∼

Ὅλην ἀναθέμενοι ἐν αὐτοῖς τὴν ἐλπί-
δα, θησαυρὸν ἀσύλητον ἑαυτοῖς οἱ ἅ-
γιοι ἐθησαύρισαν· δωρεὰν ἔλαβον· δωρεὰν δίδωσι τοῖς νοσοῦσι τὰ ἰάματα·
χρυσὸν ἢ ἄργυρον εὐαγγελικῶς οὐκ ἐκ-
τήσαντο· ἀνθρώποις δὲ & κτήνεσι τὰς εὐεργεσίας μετέδωκαν· ἵνα διὰ πάντων
ὑπήκοοι γενόμενοι χῶ· ἐν παρρησία
πρεσβεύωσιν ὑπὲρ τῶν ψυχῶν ἡμῶν·
ὅμοιον·

Ὅλην ἐβδελύξαντο τὴν ἐπὶ γῆς φθειρο-
μένην ἀπόλαυσιν πολῖται δὲ ἐν σαρκὶ ἰσάγγε-
λοι ἐχρημάτισαν· ἡ ὁμόφρων συσκη-
νος· ἐν νοερὸς ὁμότροπος· τῶν ἁγίων &
ὁμόψυχος· διὸ τοῖς κάμνουσι, πᾶσι τὰς
ἰάσεις βραβεύουσιν ἀνάργυρον παρέ-
χοντας· τὴν εὐεργεσίαν τοῖς χρήζου-
σιν· οὓς ἐν ἐτησίοις· τιμήσωμεν ἀξίως
ἑορταῖς· ἐν παρρησία πρεσβεύοντας·
ὑπὲρ τῶν ψυχῶν ἡμῶν :∼ ὅμοιον·

Ὅλην εἰσοικήσαντο ἐν ἑαυτῆ τὴν φιάδα
δυὰς ἡ ἀοίδιμος· κοσμᾶς & δαμιανὸς
οἱ θεόφρονα· ὡς κρουνοὶ βλύζουσιν
ἐκ πηγῶν νάματα· ζωηφόρα τῶν ἰάσε-
ων· ὧν & τὰ λείψανα πάθη διαφῆς

θεραπεύουσι· καὶ νόσα τὰ ὀνόματα·
νόσοις ἐκβροτῶν ἀπελαύνουσι· πάντων τῶν προσφύγων· σωτήριοι τελοῦν-
ται τῷ χῶ· ἐν παρρησία πρεσβεύσιμ·
ὑπὲρ τῶν ψυχῶν ἡμῶν. Δὰ τὸρον
τὰ αὐτά· δόξα· ἦχ΄ πλ β. αὐτόπολίν·

Ἀτελεύτητος ὑπάρχει τῶν ἁγίων ἡ χά-
εις· ἣν παρὰ χῦ ἐκομίσαντο· ὅθεν αὐ-
τῶν καὶ τὰ λείψανα ἐκ θείας δυνάμε-
ως, διηνεκῶς ἐνεργοῦσι τοῖς θαύμασιν·
ὧν καὶ τὰ ὀνόματα μόνα· ἐκ πίστεως
ἐπιβοώμενα· τῶν ἀνιάτων ἀλγηδό-
νων ἀπαλλάττουσι· δι᾽ ὧν κέ & ἡμᾶς·
τῶν τῆς ψυχῆς καὶ σώματος παθῶν ἐ-
λευθέρωσον ὡς φιλάνθρωπος. & νῦν &·
θεοτοκίον κέ σὺ εἶ ἡ ἄμπελος ἡ ἀληθινὴ προσ-
ρώσασε σταυρούμενον· χ' ἡ σὲ κινήσασα·
ἀνεβόα· τί ὁ ἐξ ἐμοῦ ὁ ἐρῶ μυστήριον ὑέ
μου· πῶς ἐπὶ ξύλου θνήσκεις· σαρκὶ
κρεμάμενος ζωῆς χορηγέ. Εἰ βούλει
ἑορτάσαι εἶπε ἀναγνώσματα μαρτυ-
ρικὰ· ζήτει κζ τῷ αὐτῷ μηνός· εἶτα
ψάλλε εἰς τὴν λιτὴν, τὰ παρόντα ἀλ
ἦχ΄ πλ β.

Πηγὴ τῶν ἰαμάτων, ἕνα & μόνον ἔθε-

elected chaplain of San Giorgio dei Greci, the church of the Greek community of Venice.

Nikolaos Malaxos was born in Nauplia, in the Peloponnese. He came from a well-known family of learned churchmen and had studied at the Patriarchal Academy in Constantinople. In 1538 he was ordained *Protopapas* of Nauplia, the highest office allowed to the Orthodox clergy by the Venetian authorities. The position of Metropolitan had been abolished by the Venetians. Malaxos and his family fled to Crete when Nauplia fell to the Turks on 21 November 1540. He then went to Venice, where he earned a living by copying manuscripts. At one time he belonged to the Scriptorium of Guillaume Pellicier, bishop of Montpellier who was the French ambassador to Venice. During his stay in Venice Pellicier had manuscripts copied on behalf of his king, Francis I. Malaxos also worked as editor and corrector of liturgical books for Andrea Spinelli. From the epistle of Eparchos to Patriarch Dionysios we know that Malaxos was responsible for the preparation of the texts of the *Μηναῖα*.

The woodcut of the Crucifixion surrounded by cuts of religious scenes found in this work was originally used in a *Missale romanum* of 1521 printed by Lucantonio Giunti. The initials *LVNF* stand for a little-known artist who also signed some of his works as *Lunardus* or *Leonardus*. His work is found in several Catholic religious books published by Lucantonio Giunti.

1983 – Harry Knowles Messenger and Ada Messenger Fund.

5. [Θεῖαι Λειτουργεῖαι] Συναγῶβον, παρὰ Ἀνθίμου Ἱερομονάχου τοῦ ἐξ Ἰβηρίας, 1701.

This work contains the liturgies of the Orthodox Church, the offices for Matins and Vespers, and other services in Greek and Arabic. It was printed at the request of Athanasios IV Dabbas, Patriarch of Antioch who, on a trip to Rumania about 1700, had requested the help of the Voivode Constantin Brâncoveanu (1688 – 1714) in printing some liturgical books in Arabic for the Orthodox Christian Arabs of Syria.

The printer Antim of Ivir, was able to design and cut Arabic type and at least two works were printed in the two languages, the first in 1701 at the monastery of Snagov near Bucharest. This is the present book. It was followed by the publication in Bucharest of an Ὡρολόγιον or Book of Hours in 1702. After the publication of these two books it is believed that the Arabic type was given to the Patriarch Athanasios, who took it with him to Aleppo where he inaugurated a series of Arabic publications that lasted until his death in 1724.

Antim of Ivir, an Orthodox monk (*hieromonachos*) from Georgia (Iviria) was the most important printer of Greek in Rumania. He printed in various places, taking his press wherever his ecclesiastical duties took him: in Bucharest from 1691 to 1694, Snagov from 1696 to 1701, when he was the Abbot of the monastery there, and in Bucharest again between 1701-1705. In 1705 Antim became Bishop of Rimnic in Oltenia and printed there in 1705 and 1706. He became Metropolitan of Wallachia in 1709 and he and his press moved to Tirgoviste, the old capital of Wallachia. Books were printed by him in Tirgoviste between 1709 and 1715. The last book with his name was printed in 1716, the year of his death in Bucharest.

The liturgies are printed in red and black, the traditional way of printing Greek liturgical books. This book is illustrated with seven woodcuts: the arms of Wallachia, a raven holding a cross in his beak, and woodcuts of Christ Pantocrator, Saint John Chrysostom, Saint Gregorias, and Christ in the Eucharistic chalice.

1974 – Duplicates from the bequest of J. H. Schaffner

Η ΘΕΙΑ ΛΕΙΤΟΥΡΓΙΑ,

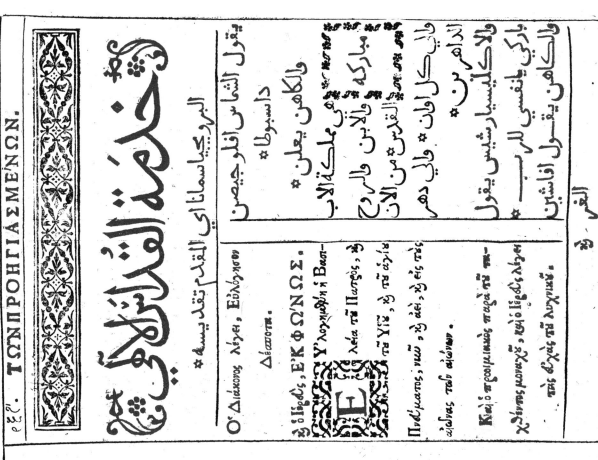

ΤΩΝ ΠΡΟΗΓΙΑΣΜΕΝΩΝ.

البركة كالعادة الى القداس

* يسجد ثلاثا*

Ο Διάκονος λέγει, Εὐλόγησον

Δέσποτα.

Ὁ Ἱερεὺς, ΕΚΦΩΝΩΣ.

Εὐλογημένη ἡ Βασι-

λεία τοῦ Πατρὸς, ᾧ
τοῦ Υἱοῦ, ᾧ τοῦ Ἁγίου
Πνεύματος, νῦν, ᾧ ἀεὶ, ᾧ εἰς τοὺς
αἰῶνας τῶν αἰώνων.

Καὶ ὁ προεστὼς παρὰ τοῦ οἰκ

يقول الشماس القربة
* دسيوطا يعلي

الأكهين ... بركة يا سيد

الكاهن يقول القانون ...

والكاهن ...

الدائمين *

6. Ὀκτώηχος. Ἐνετίῃσι, παρὰ Νικολάῳ Γλυκεῖ τῷ ἐξ Ἰωαννίνων 1701.

The Ὀκταώηχος is the liturgical book that contains the hymns pertaining to eight consecutive Sundays, one for each *echos* or mode. Some of the hymns contained in the *Oktoechos* are attributed to Saint John of Damaskos and in many of the early printed editions one can find a woodcut representing the saint sitting at his desk writing. The *Oktoechos* was first printed in Rome in 1520 by Zacharias Kalliergis and since that time it came out regularly every few years. Besides its use as a liturgical book it was also used along with the Psalter and the *Horologion* as a schoolbook during the years of the Turkish Occupation. Thus as early as 1549 we find pocket editions of the *Oktoechos* displaying a schoolbook scene on the lower part of the titlepage. Some time in the late sixteenth century the cut with the school scene was tranferred to the top of the second leaf, as is the case with this edition of the *Oktoechos*. It has all the characteristic features found in the fifteenth century editions, such as the printing in red and black, the cut of Saint John of Damaskos (A2v) and also two other illustrations, one of the Crucifixion (G8v) and the other of the Resurrection (O8r). Nearly every edition of the *Oktoechos* since the second edition of 1523 displays these features.

The 1701 Ὀκτώηχος was published in Venice by the firm of Nikolaos Glykys who was from Ioannina in Epirus. On the titlepage there is the famous Glykys mark, a bee. Nikolaos Glykys founded his printing firm in 1670 and it lasted until 1854, thus making it the longest running Greek publishing firm of the Tourkokratia. Between 1670 and 1854 the Glykys firm printed some two thousand Greek books.

6

1971 – Duplicate Fund.

7. Ἀκολουθία τοῦ ἐν ἀγίοις πατρὸς ἡμῶν Βησσαρίωνος. Ἐν Μοσχοπόλει, παρὰ Γρηγορίῳ ἱερομονάχῳ τῷ Κωνσταντινίδη 1744.

This is the Office (Ἀκολουθία) of Saint Bessarion the miracle-maker (Θαυματουργός), archbishop of Larissa. The service of Saint Bessarion was translated into modern Greek and was first printed in Bucharest by Anthimos of Ivir in 1705. The present edition was printed in Moschopolis (Voskopje, Albania) in northern Epirus. Its printing was subsidized by the metropolitan of Larissa Iakovos and the abbot of the monastery of Dousiko.

The Moschopolis press was active between 1731 and c. 1760. During this period Moschopolis was a thriving commercial and cultural center, and also boasted an academy or school of higher learning. The aims of the Moschopolis press were confined to the region; most of the books printed were service-books of neomartyrs and local saints, although at least two works were printed in order to counteract the proselytizing by the Catholics of the region. The printer in charge was Georgios Konstantinides who later also taught at the Academy.

By far the most controversial book printed by the Moschopolis press was Ἡ ἀλήθεια κριτής of father

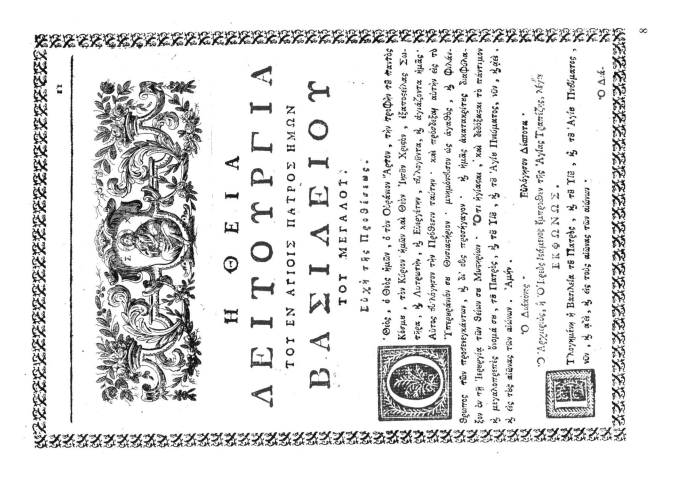

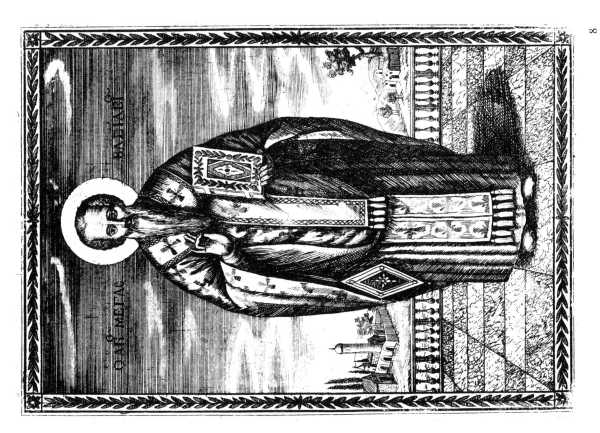

Ventzonis, an Italian Jesuit converted to the Orthodox faith. The book is a polemic against both the Catholic and the Calvinist doctrines.

One of the characteristics of the imprints of this press is the charm of the woodcut illustrations and initials, which, although reminiscent of Venetian ornamental woodblocks, manage to combine the freshness and primitive charm of the folk traditions of the region.

1980 – Duplicate Fund.

8. Ἀρχιερατικὸν περιέχον τὰς θείας καὶ ἱερὰς Λειτουργίας . . . Ἐν Κωνσταντινουπόλει, Ἐν τῷ κατὰ τὰ Πατριαρχεῖα Ἑλληνικῷ Τυπογραφείῳ 1820.

The *Archieratikon* contains the liturgies of Saint Chrysostom, of Saint Basil the Great and of Saint Gregory Dialogos, i.e. the liturgy of the Presanctified. In addition, it includes the ceremonies and services for all ordinations as well as the betrothal and marriage services. Thus the *Archieratikon* consists of the parts of the service contained in the *Euchologion* which is performed by the *Archiereus*, i.e. a bishop or higher. As a separate liturgical book, the *Archieratikon* was first printed in Paris in 1643.

This folio edition of the *Archieratikon* was printed by the third Patriarchal press of Constantinople (1798 – 1821). It is printed in red and black throughout and is illustrated with an engraved headpiece and decorative initials. It also contains two full-page engravings of Saint Basil and Saint Gregory Dialogos. On the titlepage, instead of a printer's mark, there is a small cut on the Last Supper. This copy has an exceptionally fine original binding.

1977 – Duplicate Fund.

Orthodox Church

After the Turkish conquest of Byzantium the Orthodox Church was the only Byzantine institution that was not dismantled and was allowed to continue to function. Sultan Mehmet II, following the traditional pattern employed by other Muslim conquerors, allowed each religious minority under his rule to organize as a *milet*, or nation. Thus, the first Patriarch of Constantinople after the conquest, Gennadios Scholarios (c. 1400 –c. 1468), became both the religious leader and Ethnarch of the Greek nation. Besides his religious duties, the Patriarch and by extension the metropolitans and other prelates became responsible and served as arbiters in matters of marriage and divorce, wills, legacies, minor infractions and misdemeanors.

In the field of education the churches' contribution was immense. After the fall of Constantinople the university was closed and most scholars and professors left for the West. Only the Patriarchal Academy remained open and it devoted itself to the training and education of the clergy. In the rest of the country conditions were deplorable. In his *Germanograecia*, Martinus Crusius (1526–1607), Professor of Greek at Tübingen, writes of the pitiful state of Greek education and the lack of schools. Gradually and with the financial help of the Greek communities of the Diaspora there was a change and schools were founded in various parts of Greece.

Most of the Greeks who wanted to study in schools of higher learning had to travel abroad, to Venice and especially to the University of Padua which was not under Papal influence. Many Orthodox clerics were educated at Padua. Among them Maximos Margounios, Bishop of Kythera, Gabriel Severos, Archbishop of Philadelphia, Nikephoros Parasches, Vicar to the Patriarch Hieremias II, Kyrillos Loukaris, Patriarch of Constantinople, Meletios Pegas, Patriarch of Alexandria, and many, many others. In 1593 the Patriarch of Constantinople Hieremias II convened a Synod to write a new constitution for the Patriarchal Academy and to introduce new subjects in its curriculum, such as philosophy and certain of the sciences, theology, and literature. It was during this time that other academies were founded in Thessaloniki, Trebizond, Smyrna, and elsewhere. The Patriarch Hieremias also asked all Metropolitans to establish and run schools attached to their Metropolitan Sees. The Patriarch Kyrillos Loukaris invited the distinguished Aristotelian philosopher Theophilos Korydalleus to head the Patriarchal Academy and revise its curriculum. Chrysanthos Notaras, Patriarch of Jerusalem was instrumental in helping to establish the Greek academies of Bucharest and Jassy at the beginning of the eighteenth century. Virtually all the teachers during the years of the Turkish Occupation came from the ranks of the clergy. Thus the Orthodox Church and its clergy were truly the teachers of the nation.

9. Alexios Rhartouros, c. 1504–1574. Διδαχαί. Ἐνετίῃσιν, ἐν οἰκίᾳ ἀλεξίου ἱερέως τοῦ ῥαρτούρου 1560.

Alexios Rhartouros was a cleric who bore the title *Chartophylax* of Corfu as is given on the titlepage of his sermons. He belonged to a well-established family of the island. His father was Aloïsios Rhartouros, who was *Protopapas* of Corfu and with whom he is sometimes confused in the sources. It was Alexios and not his father who was sent to Rome in 1538 to request on behalf of the Orthodox clergy of the island the intercession of Pope Paul III against the abuses of the Latin bishops. And indeed in 1540 a new papal Bull was issued reaffirming the privileges accorded to the Orthodox given by Pope Leo X (1513–1521).

Alexios Rhartouros made several trips to Venice and in 1559 applied for a license to print his sermons, which came out in 1560. The sermons were written in modern Greek, which is significant. Up until this time

ΔΙΔΑΧΑΙ ΑΛΕΞΙΟΥ

ΙΕΡΕΏΣ ΤΟΥ ΡΑΡΤΟΥΡΟΥ ΚΑΙ ΧΑΡΤΟ-
φύλακος κερκύρας τουτὶ τὸ βιβλίον καλεῖται. ἐπειδὴ περιέχει ἐν
ἑαυτῷ, τὰς ἰδίας αὐτῇ διδαχὰς ὑπὸ καθ᾿ εἱρμὸν καὶ τάξιν διῃρημέ
νας δι᾿ ρυθμῶς καὶ τεχνικῶς σωτοῖς αὐτῇ προοιμίοις ἢ δικοῖς τε
καὶ ὑπιλόγοις. καὶ ἑρμηνευθείσας παρ᾿ αὐτ᾿ εἰς κοινὴν διάλεκτον
προς μεγίστην ὠφέλειαν παντὸς τῆ χριστωνύμου λαῆ.

Χάλεπι τῆς ἐκλαμπροτάτης ἀρχῆς τῇ ἐνετῇ, διαρηθείση τῷ
εἰρημένῳ ἱερεῖ δι᾿ ἐτῇ δέκα ἵνα μήτις ἕτερος τολμήση τυπω-
σαι αὐτὰς ἐν ταύτη τῆ πόλει, μήτε ἄλλοθί πω τυπωθεί
σας πωλήση ἐν τοῖς χωρίοις ταύτης τῆ ἀρχῆς. εἰ δὲ
μὴ δῶσι δίκιω χρυσίνας διακοσίας, καὶ
τ᾿ ἄλλα ὡς ἐν τῆ χάλεπι γέγραπται.

the only texts published in modern Greek were the popular literary texts that were produced for the entertainment of the people. Rhartouros was the second clergyman to use the spoken language in order to reach a wider audience. The first to do this was Damaskenos Stoudites, bishop of Lite and Rendina, who in 1558, perhaps earlier, published his sermons in modern Greek. Damaskenos' Θησαυρός became very popular and not only with the Greeks. It was also read widely among the Slavs and was reprinted regularly until the nineteenth century.

Alexios Rhartouros was elected *Protopapas* (Chief priest) of Corfu in 1572, a title he held until his death in 1574.

1962 – The gift of George L. Lincoln (HC 1895).

10. Kyrillos Loukaris, successively Patriarch of Alexandria and Constantinople, 1572 – 1638. Σύντομος πραγματεία κατὰ Ἰουδαίων ἐν ἀπλῇ διαλέκτῳ. Ἐν Κωσταντινουπόλει, Νικόδημος Μεταξᾶς 1627.

Kyrillos Loukaris was one of the most enlightened partriarchs of the *Tourkokratia* and the main figure of what is considered in Greek letters the era of religious humanism (1600 – 1669).

Loukaris was a native of Crete and was educated in Italy where his first teacher was Maximos Margounios, Bishop of Kythera. Upon completion of his studies with Margounios he entered the University of Padua. After completing his studies there he returned to Crete and shortly thereafter went to Constantinople, where he entered the priesthood. He was ordained by a kinsman, Meletios Pegas, Patriarch of Alexandria, who was in Constantinople at the time. It was during this period that the Church authorities were concerned about the fate of the Orthodox in Poland who were gradually being deprived of their religious freedom and coerced into joining the Roman Catholic Church by becoming uniates, i.e. declaring allegiance to the Pope. Kyrillos Loukaris was sent twice to Poland as Exarch (special envoy) of the Patriarchate of Alexandria. In the Orthodox Brotherhoods (*bratstva*) he visited (Vilna and Lvov) he reformed and reorganized the schools run by the Orthodox priests.

Upon the death of Meletios Pegas in 1601 Kyrillos Loukaris was elected Patriarch of Alexandria and then of Constantinople in 1612. These were greatly turbulent years for the Orthodox Church, a time in which the Catholic Church made a concerted effort to attract and proselytize the Orthodox by establishing well-run and well-equipped Catholic schools in various parts of Greece. The efforts of the Catholic Church were aided by the Catholic ambassadors in Constantinople who spent large sums of money for this purpose. Kyrillos Loukaris re-organized the Patriarchal Academy and appointed an old class-mate from Padua, Theophilos Korydalleus, to head it. He was also aided in his efforts to counteract the Catholic attacks on

himself by the ambassadors of the Protestant countries, mainly the English and the Dutch, with whom he formed lasting friendships. Through contacts with Sir Thomas Roe, Ambassador of Great Britain, he began a correspondence with George Abbot, Archbishop of Canterbury. Abbot invited Loukaris to send some Orthodox priests to be educated in England and in 1617 he sent one Metrophanes Kritopoulos from Veroia in Macedonia, who spent five years at Balliol College at Oxford. It was during the time that Metrophanes Kritopoulos was in England that another Greek priest, the Hieromonachos Nikodemos Metaxas of Cephalonia (1585 – 1646), went to England to join his brother, a merchant in London, and to further his education. It seems that Metaxas was interested in learning the art of printing and was actively doing so in London. When Metrophanes reported this to the Patriarch, Loukaris sent to Metrophanes some manuscripts to be printed by Metaxas. These included treatises by Meletios Pegas, Gennadios Scholarios, Neilos Kabasilas, Georgios Koresios, Maximos Margounios, and Barlaam the Monk, all disputing the supremacy of the Pope. These tracts were printed by Metaxas in England without indication of place or date of publication and were carried by him along with equipment to set up a press in Constantinople.

Metaxas arrived in Constantinople in June 1627 and set up his press but was able to print only one tract, consisting of two works: Loukaris' Σύντομος πραγματεία κατὰ Ἰουδαίων and the Ὁμιλίαι of Maximos Margounios. Although the place and date of publication of this tract is given as Constantinople, 1627, there is documentary evidence from reports of the English Ambassador, Sir Thomas Roe and the Bailo of Venice, Sebastiano Venier, that the Loukaris work was actually printed in England and the sheets brought to Constantinople where the Ὁμιλίαι of

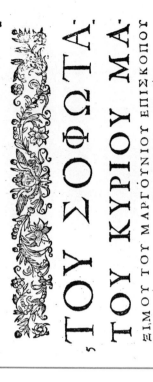

ΤΟΥ ΣΟΦΩΤΑ-
ΤΟΥ ΚΥΡΙΟΥ ΜΑ-
ΞΙΜΟΥ ΤΟΥ ΜΑΡΓΟΥΝΙΟΥ ΕΠΙΣΚΟΠΟΥ

ΠΡΟΟΙΜΙΟΝ.

ΤΟΥ ΜΑΚΑΡΙΩ-
ΤΑΤΟΥ ΚΑΙ ΣΟΦΩ-
ΤΑΤΟΥ ΠΑΤΡΟΣ ΗΜΩΝ ΠΑΠΑ ΚΑΙ ΠΑ-

ΚΥΡΙΛΛΟΥ

Margounios were printed to complete the tract. The Turkish authorities seized the press as soon as the tract circulated and nothing more was printed in Constantinople.

Kyrillos wrote a Confession of Faith which was printed in Latin in Geneva in 1629. The Greek text along with the Latin translation was published also in Geneva in 1633. This Confession of Faith of Kyrillos Loukaris rocked both the Orthodox and Catholic Churches because it was considered to be closer to Calvinist than to Orthodox doctrine, and it was repudiated by the Orthodox Church. Loukaris also commissioned the publication of the first modern Greek translation of the New Testament made by Maximos Kallipolites which was printed in Geneva in 1638. Kyrillos Loukaris was put to death by the Turks in 1638.

1970 – Friends of the Harvard College Library and the Harry Knowles Messenger and Ada Messenger Fund.

11. Dositheos, Patriarch of Jerusalem, 1641 – 1707. Ἱστορία τῶν περὶ τῶν ἐν Ἱεροσολύμοις πατριαρχευσάντων. Ἐν Βουκουρεστίῳ τῆς Οὐγγροβλαχίας, ἐπιστατοῦντος τῇ τυπογραφίᾳ Στώϊκα ἱερέως τοῦ Ἰακωβίτζῃ 1715.

Dositheos was born in Arachova, a village near Corinth in the Peloponnese. His father died when he was about eight, and his upbringing and education was taken over by his grandfather and his godfather, the Metropolitan of Corinth Gregorios Galanos. Dositheos entered the church at an early age, becoming an hierodiakonos and soon afterwards, in 1656, went to Constantinople, where, he studied under Nikolaos Kerameus. It was during his stay in Constantinople that Dositheos met and came under the aegis of the Patriarch of Jerusalem Païsios, with whom he travelled extensively throughout the Orthodox world. After Païsios' death in 1660, Dositheos was attached to the newly elected Patriarch of Jerusalem Nektarios (1660–1669). Again he travelled with the Patriarch and also acted on his behalf as Exarch to raise money in order to pay the huge debt owed by the patriarchate of Jerusalem to the Turkish authorities for their allowing the maintenance of the Holy Land. In 1666 he was consecrated Metropolitan of Caesaria and when in 1669 Nektarios resigned as Patriarch because of old-age and ill-health, Dositheos was elected Patriarch of Jerusalem at the age of twenty-eight.

The years of Dositheos' patriarchate were turbulent ones for the Orthodox Church. Besides the struggle among the Orthodox, the Catholics and the Armenians to gain the upper hand in the administration of the Holy monuments in Palestine, there was also the struggle by the Orthodox Church to fight the propaganda assaults of the Catholic Church and the Jansenists, who were very active in the Eastern Mediterranean trying to convert the Orthodox to their cause. In his efforts to obtain favorable conditions for the Orthodox Church in the administration of the Christian monuments of Palestine Dositheos was greatly helped by the Phanariot Alexandros Mavrokordatos the Exaporite, who was the Grand Dragoman of the Sultan. It was Mavrokordatos who repeatedly persuaded the Turkish authorities to rule in favor of the Orthodox Church. Dositheos was also very active and influential among the ruling princes of Moldavia and Wallachia in the Danubian principalities, where he spent much time in his travels to raise money for the patriarchate. It was during one of his visits to Jassy in Moldavia in 1680, that he observed printing presses in operation undisturbed by the authorities and conceived the idea of installing a Greek press there. Dositheos himself gives us particulars of his visit and actions in his Ἱστορία. He recounts that he gave the monk Mitrofan 600 piasters in order to purchase Greek type and also provided funds for paper and other necessary equipment and wages. Dositheos also sent Mitrofan the manuscript of his predecessor, the Patriarch Nektarios, against the primacy of the Pope which was the first work to be printed. Thus in 1682 a Greek press began to operate at the monastery of Cetatsuia outside Jassy. Later, in 1690 he was instrumental in also establishing a Greek press in Bucharest.

The presses of Jassy and Bucharest and later those of Snagov, Rîmnic, and Tîrgoviste published much of the Orthodox dogmatic and anti-Catholic literature that could not be printed in Catholic Venice.

Dositheos' Ἱστορία also known as the Δωδεκάβιβλος was published posthumously and edited by his nephew and successor to the patriarchal see of Jerusalem, Chrysanthos Notaras. Dositheos' work is a chronicle of the history of the Orthodox Church, especially of the Patriarchate of Jerusalem and the Holy Land, and in particular of Dositheos' own patriarchate.

1971 – Friends of the Harvard College Library and the Harry Knowles Messenger and Ada Messenger Fund.

ΠΑΤΡΙΑΡΧΗΣ

Η ΑΓΙΑΣ ΠΟΛΕΩΣ ΙΕΡΟΥΣΑΛΗΜ

ΕΛΕΩ ΘΕΟΥ

ΔΟΣΙΘΕΟΣ

12. Chrysanthos Notaras, Patriarch of Jerusalem, c. 1663–1731. Εἰσαγωγή εἰς τὰ γεωγραφικὰ καὶ σφαιρικά. Ἐν Παριουίοις, 1716.

Chrysanthos Notaras, who was from the Peloponnese, was related on his mother's side to the Patriarch of Jerusalem, Dositheos. His education was taken over by Dositheos, and he and his brother Neophytos were sent to Constantinople to study at the Patriarchal Academy. There he was the pupil of Sevastos Kymenites, who taught Aristotelian philosophy. At the time Chrysanthos was a deacon. By 1684 Chrysanthos had already been sent on various missions on behalf of the Patriarchate of Jerusalem, especially to the principalities of Moldavia and Wallachia. In 1693 he was sent to Moscow, again on behalf of Dositheos, where he stayed until 1696. It was during his stay in Russia that he wrote a work on China, entitled *Kitaïa douleuousa*, using as his source the Tsar's representative to China, Nikolaos Spathar Milescu. After his return from Russia Chrysanthos went to further his studies in Europe. He first visited Vienna and then went to Venice and by 1697 he was studying at the University of Padua. In 1700 Chrysanthos went to Paris where he studied with the astronomer Giovanni-Domenico Cassini among others.

In 1701 he was again sent to Russia by Patriarch Dositheos to deliver a message to Peter the Great concerning the custodianship of the Holy Places. On his return from Russia he stopped at Bucharest, where he became the tutor of the children of Alexandros Mavrokordatos with whom both he and Dositheos maintained very close ties. In April 6, 1702 he was consecrated Metropolitan of Caesaria and Palestine. Upon the death of Dositheos in 1707 the Synod elected him Patriarch of Jerusalem.

Like his predecessor, Chrysanthos was a very active Patriarch and was always travelling to collect money in order to maintain and restore the Holy Places. Among his many writings both in print and in manuscript form there survives a diary of the trips he undertoook between 1720 and 1726. It gives information about the various churches and congregations visited. Chrysanthos was one of the most learned Patriarchs of the eighteenth century. He left a voluminous oeuvre and correspondence and a rich personal library, some of which formed part of the library of the Patriarchate of Jerusalem.

His treatise on Geography was commissioned and financed by Ioannis Nikolaou Mavrokordatos, Voivode of Wallachia (1670–1730).

Early acquisition – Source unknown.

13. Βιβλίον περιέχον τὴν Ἀκολουθίαν τῆς Ἁγίας Αἰκατερίνης. Ἐνετίησι, παρὰ Νικολάῳ τῷ Σάρῳ 1727.

This Προσκυνητάρι contains the office of Saint Catharine of Mount Sinai, the description of Mount Sinai and its surroundings, history of the monastery, and a list of its past prelates. The work was commissioned by Nikephoros Marthales Glykys, the Abbot of the monastery of the Holy Prodromos in Constantinople. The Prodromos monastery was a dependency (μετόχι) of Saint Catharine's. The work was edited and corrected by Marinos Pieros of Corfu and published in Venice by the Nikolaos Saros publishing house.

Nikolaos Saros was an Epeirote publisher active in Venice during the seventeenth century. The Saros press began its operations in 1681 but when Nikolaos Saros died in 1697, neither of his two sons were trained as printers and the printing establishment passed into the hands of Antonio Bortoli in 1706 or 1707. However, Bortoli was under obligation to use the Saros name and mark until 1778 when the whole sum owed the Saros family for the purchase of the press and its equipment was completely paid up.

The above book is a special type of guide-book written for the use of those wishing to make a pilgrimage to the important monasteries of the Orthodox world and the Holy Land. They included not only descriptions of the places to be visited but the Office (Ἀκολουθία) of the saint to whom the monastery was dedicated and other pertinent information, such as legends connected with them, illustrations of the Saint, and prayers and devotions to be used during the visits. There is a fairly large collection of these travel books, known as Προσκυνητάρια which have survived both in manuscript and printed form. The most popular monasteries to visit after the Holy places in Palestine were the monasteries on Mount Athos, the monastery of the Zoodochos Pege in Constantinople and the Kykko monastery on the island of Cyprus which was supposed to have an icon painted by Saint Luke.

1900 – From the library of Count Paul Riant (Gift of John Harvey Treat of Lawrence).

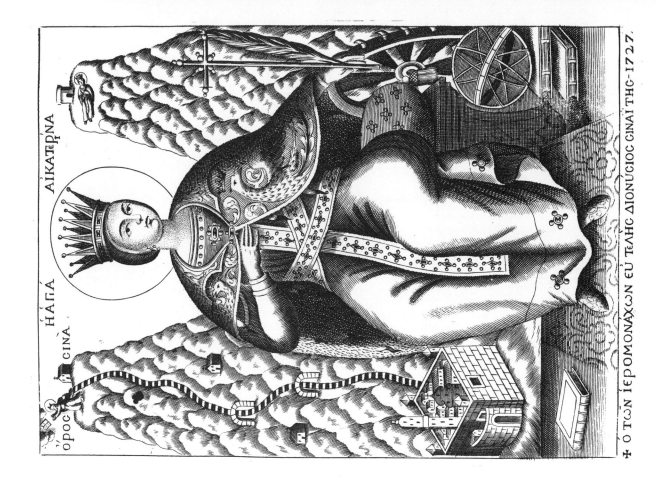

ΠΡΟΟΙΜΙΟΝ

PRAEFATIO

ΠΡΟΟΙΜΙΟΝ

Τοῖς ἐντευξομένοις γνησίοις τέκνοις τῆς Ἁγίας τοῦ Χριστοῦ Ἐκκλησίας, χαίρειν.

Ἔθος ἐστὶν ἄνωθεν τῇ τῶν Ὀρθοδόξων Ἐκκλησία προνοεῖν ὑπὲρ τῶν ἐκκλινόντων ἐξ ὁδοῦ δικαίας εἰς παρεκτροπὴν δογμάτων. ὅθεν καὶ νῦν τῇ συνήθει χρωμένη προνοίᾳ, ἠξίωσε συγγράψαι ταύτην τὴν Βίβλον, σαφῶς δεικνύουσαν τό, τε ἀληθὲς τοῦ Θείου Βαπτίσματος, καὶ τὸ ψεῦδος τοῦ παππικὰ βαντίσματος, μήποτε εἰς ἀπόπτωσιν ἐλθόντες οἱ Λατῖνοι δυνηθῶσι γνῶναι, ἕως χαλεπῶς δρακων ἔχυσεν αὐτὲς κατεπάτει· ταῦτα τὸν γὰρ νῦν συνήθη Λατῖνοις παθεῖν, ὅπερ φαίνεται συμβὰν ποτε τοῖς Ἰουδαίοις, πλανωμένοις ἐν τῇ ἐρήμῳ· Ἀριθμ. Κεφ. κά. καθάπερ γὰρ τότε ἐκεί-

PRAEFATIO

Lecturis genuinis filiis sanctae Christi ecclesiae salutem.

Vetus ecclesiae orthodoxorum mos est prospicere semperde iis qui recta de via ad dogmatum erronea itinera declinaverunt. Ideo nunc familiari usa circumspectione hunc conscribere librum voluit qui veritatem diuini baptismatis et mendacium papisticae adspersionis luculenter demonstrabit, vt aliquando tandem latini sensibus receptis scire possint quam difficilis draco deglutire ipsos potuerit. Idem enim nunc latinis accidit quod judaeis olim in deserto errantibus. Num. c. 21. Veluti enim tunc

PREFAZIONE

Ai lettori ed ai figli sinceri della S.S. Chiesa di Gesù Cristo salute.

L'uso antico della chiesa si è di ridurre alla ragione quegli, che si sono allontanati dalla retta strada, e dalla vera dottrina. Per questa ragione ho voluto scrivere questo libro colla solita precauzione, che dimostrerà chiaramente la verità del divino battesimo, e la mensogna dell' asperzione Papale, affinche i Latini finalmente illuminati sappiano con quanta facilità 'l dragone infernale avrebbe potuto assorbirli. Mentre lo stesso accade ai latini, ch'accadette altre volte agli Ebrei erranti nella solitudine. Num. cap. 21. Siccome allora Iddio

14. Βιβλίον καλούμενον Ῥαντισμοῦ στηλίτευσις. Ἐν Λιψίᾳ τῆς Σαξωνίας, Παρὰ Ἰωάννῃ Γόττλοπ Ἐμμανουὴλ Πρέϊτκοπφ 1758.

The work is the outcome of the Baptism controversy which broke out in 1750 when Cyril V, Patriarch of Constantinople insisted that members of other Christian sects should be baptized anew by immersion when converted to the Orthodox Church. This view was not only attacked by the Catholic Church but also by many of the Orthodox prelates who denounced Cyril's actions. This created a turbulent debate within the Orthodox Church. On the side of Cyril V was a theologian of note, Eustratios Argentes (c. 1687–c. 1757) of Chios, a layman educated in medicine and theology in Western Europe who was one of the best-known physicians in the Near East. According to Eustratios Argentes immersion was the only canonical form of baptism. The controversy arose because the practices of the Orthodox Church had been inconsistent in this matter through the centuries. There were three ways of receiving heretics and schismatics into the Orthodox Church. Some were received by communion without baptism, others were required to be anointed with the Holy Chrism, and yet a third

class were not only chrismated but also baptised because their previous baptism was considered invalid.

During this controversy with his Synod Cyril issued in June 1755 an encyclical written in modern Greek that was an answer to the decree issued by the Synod on April 28. Cyril's encyclical advocates rebaptism in the case of converts from the Roman and Armenian Churches and anathematizes all who accepted the Synod's decree. This anathema first appeared in the first edition of 'Ραντισμοῦστηλίτευσις that was printed in 1756 in Constantinople. The above trilingual edition in Greek, Latin and Italian was printed in Leipzig in 1758. It was printed at the expense of the Monastery of the Holy Virgin of Kykko in Cyprus and was edited by the Archimandrite Serapheim Pissidios, who was a monk at the monastery. His coat of arms appears on the titlepage of the work.

1971 – Friends of the Harvard College Library and the Harry Knowles Messenger and Ada Messenger Fund.

15. [Samouel Chantzeres, Patriarch of Constantinople, 1700–1775] Διαταγαὶ γάμων. [Ἐν Κωνσταντινουπόλει] Παρὰ Παναγιώτῃ Κυριακίδῃ τῷ βυζαντίῳ 1767.

This book does not indicate an author on its titlepage and neither does it give place of publication. However, it contains sermons on marriage and dowry given by the Patriarch Samouel Chantzeres. Samouel Chantzeres belonged to a Phanariot family of Constantinople and was educated at the Patriarchal Academy. In 1731 he was ordained Metropolitan of Derkon. He was first elected Patriarch of Constantinople in 1763 but was dethroned in 1768 by factions hostile to him, although the reasons why are not clear. He retired to Mount Athos during this period. Chantzeres was recalled to the Patriarchal throne in 1773 and remained until he resigned on 24 December 1774. He then retired to

Halki where he died and was buried at the back of the Church of Hagios Nikolaos on May 10, 1775.

From its type and ornaments the volume has been attributed to the second Patriarchal press in Constantinople. The press was active between 1756 and 1767 and three of the books, like the one displayed here, mention a Panayotis Kyriakides as the printer. From information given on the titlepage of one of the books we also know that the press operated in a building opposite the Patriarchate. The present book was the last from this second Patriarchal press.

1971 – Duplicate Fund.

16. Προσκυνητάριον τῆς Ἁγίας πόλεως Ἱερουσαλὴμ καὶ πάσης Παλαιστίνης. Ἐν Βιέννῃ, παρὰ τῷ Φράντζ Ἀντωνίῳ Σχρέμβλ 1799.

Although the first books written in *Karamanli*, i.e. Turkish written in Greek characters, were printed by the Patriarchal presses of Constantinople, soon other printers in Venice, Vienna, Leipzig and Bucharest also

began publishing them. *Karamanli* books were usually but not exclusively religious in nature and were sent to the Greeks of the Karaman region in Asia Minor who no longer spoke Greek but had retained their Orthodox

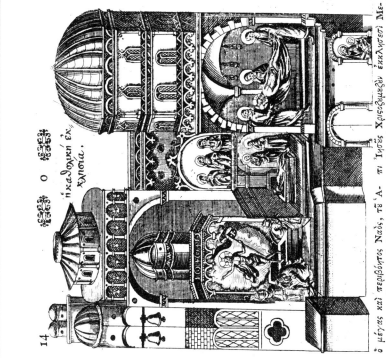

ΤΗΣ ΑΓΙΑΣ ΠΟΛΕΩΣ ΙΕΡΟΥΣΑΛΗΜ

ΑΝΘΙΜΟΣ ΕΛΕΩ ΘΕΟΥ ΠΑΤΡΙΑΡΧΕΣ

ΚΑΙ ΠΑΣΗΣ ΠΑΛΑΙΣΤΙΝΗΣ

faith and the use of the Greek alphabet. In fact, the Patriarchate of Constantinople was required by law to use *Karamanli* in all documents sent to the region. The earliest *Karamanli* printed text to have survived is a Confession of faith of the Patriarch Gennadios Scholarios (c. 1400–c. 1468) reproduced in Martinus Crusius' *Turcograeciae* in 1584.

The present edition, printed in Vienna, gives both the Greek text and *Karamanli* translation in opposite columns. It is a guide-book which describes the Christian monuments of Jerusalem and all of Palestine.

It contains several engravings of its churches, monasteries and other monuments. The Greek text was translated into *Karamanli* by Serapheim Pissidios, Metropolitan of Ankara, formerly the Abbot of the Kykko monastery in Cyprus, and was printed at the request of Anthimos, Patriarch of Jerusalem whose portrait appears as the frontispiece.

1966 – In memory of George Christos Soulis, 1927 – 1966 (Ph.D. 1958)

Diaspora

The Greeks of the Diaspora played an important role in the regeneration of the Greek nation. The first center of the Greek Diaspora after the fall of Byzantium was Venice. Greeks began to emigrate there even before 1453. Venice became the center of Greek printing for Greek readers and its university in Padua encouraged the study of Greek. A chair of Greek was founded in 1463 and its first professor was the Athenian Demetrios Chalcondyles. More Greeks received their higher education in Padua than anywhere else. Wealthy members of the Greek community of Venice financed scholarships and endowed two colleges in Padua where scholars from Greek lands could reside while studying at the university. In Venice Thomas Flanghinis left his considerable fortune for the creation of the Flaghinian School. Other wealthy Greeks left large sums of money in their wills for establishing schools in their native country. However, the greatest contribution of the Greeks of Venice was the financing and publication of an ever increasing number of books produced for export in Greek speaking lands. The Greek presses of Venice supplied Greek books to Greek readers from 1486 until 1900, long after the establishment of the Greek state in 1830.

There were many active Greek communities in other parts of Europe, in Trieste, Livorno, Amsterdam, Paris, Budapest, Odessa and elsewhere. The largest and most important in the eighteenth century was the Greek community of Vienna. It was in Vienna that the first Greek newspapers were printed as well as the first Greek journal, Ἑρμῆς ὁ Λόγιος. Most of the important books of the Greek Enlightenment were published in Vienna. Some of these books were financed by their authors or editors or by subscription, but for the most part by wealthy patrons. Among such patrons Polyzois Lambanitziotis and the five Zosimas brothers must be singled out for their great contributions to the reeducation of the Greek nation. Lambanitziotis financed some forty books between 1750 and 1796. The contribution of the Zosimas brothers was immense. They established schools and orphanages in their native Epirus and financed the publication of a series of books which were distributed free to Greek students and scholars and to those anywhere who wished to learn.

17. Ἐτυμολογικὸν μέγα. Ἐν ἐνετίαις, πόνῳ δὲ καὶ δεξιότητι Ζαχαρίου καλλιέργου τοῦ κρητός 1499.

Zacharias Kalliergis (c. 1473–1524) was born in Rethymnon, Crete and with Nikolaos Vlastos, also of Rethymnon, founded in Venice one of the most eminent Greek presses of the Renaissance run entirely by Cretans and devoted exclusively to the printing of Greek. Kalliergis' family was originally from Constantinople and claimed imperial descent. This undoubtedly accounts for his use of the double-headed eagle as his printer's mark.

The first publication of the Kalliergis-Vlastos partnership was the Ἐτυμολογικὸν μέγα of 1499. The colophon informs the reader that the work was published at the expense of Nikolaos Vlastos and at the urging of Anna Notara, the daughter of the Grand Duke of Constantinople Loukas Notaras, and that it was printed by the labor and skill of Zacharias Kalliergis. On leaf A1r there is a poem by Markos Mousouros (c. 1470–1517) which has attracted a good deal of attention because it is one of the earliest contemporary documents on the technicalities of Greek printing.

The Greek type designed and cut by Zacharias Kalliergis was fashioned after his own handwritting. The decorative initials and headpieces are reminiscent of Byzantine manuscript decorations. The woodcut borders have elaborate arabesque designs, usually white on red but also on gold. Zacharias Kalliergis was the second printer of the fifteenth century to print in gold, the first being Erhard Ratdolt. The Kalliergis decorations had a great influence on many printers, especially those who produced Greek liturgical books.

After printing four large volumes from 1499 to 1500

ΕΤΥΜΟΛΟΓΙΚΟΝ ΜΕΓΑ ΚΑΤΑ ΑΛΦΑΒΗΤΟΝ, ΠΑΝΥ ὠΦΕΛΙΜΟΝ ∴

ΤΟ ΑΛΦΑ, ΜΕΘ ΕΑΥΤΟΥ ∴

Ἄλφα τὸ στοιχεῖον, πᾶρὰ τὸ ἄλφω τὸ εὑρίσκω· πρῶτον γὰρ τῶν ἄλλων στοιχείων εὑρέθη. καὶ ἀπὸ τοῦ καλὰ ἀμοιβὰς πολιτεύεσθαι. ἀλφὴν τὴ τὰ ἀμειβήν.

Ἀαγὴς, ἄνευ ἄγης. ὅ ἐστιν ἀβλαβὴς. δύναται δὲ ὁ ὁ χαλεπὸς κỹ ὁ βλαβερὸς ἀκούεσθαι. ἴσως καὶ ἀπὸ πᾶρὰ τὴν ἐπίτασιν τοῦ ἄλφα. οὕτω μεθόδιος. ἢ ἀπὸ τοῦ ἄγω τὸ βλάπτω, ἄγα ὁ γὴς καὶ ἀαγὴς. Ἀγὴ δὲ μηρόμου σημαίνει τὴν γῆν τοῦ σούδωρ. ἢ τὸ ἀβλαβὲς, κỹ τὸ λυβλαβὲς. ἀβλαβέες μὲν, ὑγιέσιν ἐν οίκοις. πολυβλαβὲς δὲ, ὑγιέσιν ὁρκίοις.

Ἄασας, ἔβλαψας. ἐπιτάσει τοῦ ἄ. κỹ ἀασάμην, ἐβλάβην. ἀπὸ τοῦ ἄγω τὸ βλάπτω ὁμήνων, ἄσα, ὁ ἀόριστος, ἄσα. καὶ ἐπιτάσει τοῦ ἄ ἄασα. ἀᾶν ἔβλαψα. Ἀσὲ με δαίμονος ἄσα κακὴ, κỹ ἀβέσφατος οἶνος. ὁ μέσος, ἀασάμην κỹ πλεονασμῷ τοῦ δευτέρου ἀ ἀασάμην.

Ἀάσχετον, Μῆρός τι ἄνοιγος ἄεν ἀάσχετον οὐκ ἐπίσχετον. ἀπὸ τοῦ ἀκαλασχέτου, ἀκαλα κράτην, μέσα. ἀπὸ τοῦ σχῶ, σχήμι, ἔσχηκα, ἔσχεμαι, ἔσχεσαι, ἔσχεται. σχετὸς κỹ ἀσχετος. καὶ πλεονασμῷ τοῦ ἀ, ἀάσχετος.

Ἀάπτος Ὅτε κỹ χειρὸς ἀάπτους χεῖρας ἐφείω· πᾶρὰ τὸ ἄπτω· κỹ ἄπτους ἤγουν, τὰς ἀ ἀν ἀπο μῆνας· κỹ ὧν οὐκ ἄν τις ἄψαιτ. οἱονεὶ ἀπρόσ ετω. ἀπρόσπελά σοις. τὸ δὲ καθ ἀπλὸς συ πεύκησι παρα σοῦ πρὸ εὐρίται δὴ, ἐκ τοῦ καθ ἀπλὸς γέγονε καθαπὸς. οὕτω φιλόξενος ὁ δὲ ἡρωδιανὸς, τὰς μὴ διναμ᾽ ένας φθαρῆναι ἀλε ῖ σημαίνδ τὸ ὄπη, καλα σκευὰς ζωὴ οὕτως ἐστὶν ἵψ ζωὸν ἐστιν τὰ ξύλα. κỹ κλίεται ἴπως. ἐκ τοῦ τυγ μέται ῥῆμα, ἰάπτω. ξ οὗ ῥηματικὸν ὄνομα, ἰάπτος κỹ καλας᾽ έχειν. ἀΐάπτους. κỹ κατ ἔλλιψιν τοῦ ρὶ, ἀάπτους. οἱ μ̂ οὖν δασύνοὖ τὴν δευτέραν, ἀπο δ᾽ ἰδόντες ἀπροσπελάσους. οἱ δὲ ψιλοῖσιν, ἀ ἀπ τοις. ἄμοιβαὶ, ἀνεθῖκτως. ἢ χαλεπῶς. ἴ αὐ ὴ ρ᾽ μ᾿ πρῶτον, ἐκτεταμένον. τὸ δὲ δεύτερον, συνεσταλμένον.

Ἀαγὲς, ἄθραυστον. ἀπὸ τοῦ ἄγω τὸ κλάω, ἀγὴς. κỹ μετὰ τοῦ ἐπιτατικοῦ ἄλφα, ἀαγῆς. τοὺδ᾽ έτερον, ἀαγὲς. ἢ ἄθραυσον κỹ ϛ᾽ ἐκπλὴ, ἢ τὸ πολύθραυστον ∴

ΤΟ ΑΛΦΑ, ΜΕΤΑ ΤΟΥ ΒΗΤΑ ∴

Ἄβαλ, ἐπίρρημα. πᾶρὰ τὸ βάλλω. κỹ ἀφαιρέσιν τοῦ λ ϛ᾽ τοῦ ω. καὶ μὲ δὰ τοῦ ἐπιτατικοῦ ἄλφα, ἄβαλ. καὶ ἄβελ, πᾶρὰ βάλε ἐπίρρημα. ὅς τ᾽ Ἀβά λεσοι ϛ᾽ έφανε. ἀθολολά ὴ νοσαι.

Ἄβαξ, κυρίως ὁ μὴ ἔχων βάσιν. κỹ χρηστικῶς δὲ, καὶ ὡ᾽ οἵας δήποτε σανίδος. οὕτως ὡρίων. γίνεται, δὲ πᾶρὰ τῷ βῷ τῷ βαίνω.

Ἀβαρνίδα. οἷον, Περκώτην δ᾽ ὧ τὴ, καὶ ἀβαρνίδα ἡμαθόεσσαν. περκώτη δὲ ἐστι πόλις Τροίας. ἀβαρνὶς δὲ, πόλις λαμψάνου. ὠνομάθη δὲ ἀπὸ ρίαυ τῆς ἀφίας. Διονύσου ἐρασθεῖσα ἀφοδ᾽ τη, ἐμίγη αὐτῷ ἀναχωρήσαντος δὲ τοῦ τοῦ ϛ᾽ τὴν μηδ᾽ κὴν, ἐγαμήθη ἀθ᾽ μιδ᾿. ὡς δὲ ἢ λθεν ὁ διόνυσος, ϛ᾽ έφανον ποιήσασα, ἀπὴγιπσεν αὐτῷ. ἢ δ᾽ ἐπ δὲ ἀκολουθῆσαι αὐτῶ διὰ τὸ γεγαμῆσθαι. ἐς δὲ λαμψανον ἀναχωρήσασα, ἢν ἐξ ἄλλου κυοφορούμενον ἐβούλ γ᾽ ανελεῖν. ἢ δὲ ἑαρ ξύλο τυπήσασα, μεμαιευμένη τῆ χειρὶ ἐφ᾿ σαρ τῆς γαστρὸς αὐτῆς. κỹ ἐποίησεν αὐτὴν τεκεῖν παῖδα, ὃν πείθ τοῦ ὀνομαθῆναι, ἄσχημον, καὶ βαθυαιδόιον κỹ τοῦ φρ ἀπ᾿ ρήσασθαι αὐτὴν τὴν ἀφοδ᾿ την. καὶ ἀπὸ τοῦ τ̣ου, ἀπ ν᾿ ι δηκληθῆναι κỹ δι σννανάγη τοῦ σοι χεῖ᾿, ἀβαρνίδην. οὕτως ὡρος ὁ θηβαῖος ϛ᾽ έτυμ˅ λ΄γος. τὸ ἐθνικὸν ἀβαρναῖος. κỹ θηλυκῶν ἀβαρναὶν.

Ἄβάκησαν, ἢν ἠ γνόησαν. ἔστι δὲ ἡ λέξις, ἰωνρικὴ. οἱ γὰρ δ᾿ ἰκελος κỹ ἐλυθῶν πόλιν. οἱ δ᾿ ἀβάκησαν. σημαίνει δὲ καὶ ϛ᾽ ἡσου έτησαν. τὰ ἐν ἄφοις δὲ τὸ ἡσου χασαν. ἐσ βάτ᾿ ϛ᾿ λείπω. ὃ τᾶ̄ ρ᾿ ἀπ᾿ τοῦ βοά ζωκῦτ᾿ συγκοπὴν γίνεται. ὁ πάθητικὸς πᾶρ ακείμενος, βέβα κται. οἱ ϛ᾿ ἔπος δ᾿ εἴπῃ τι βέβακ ται. ϛ᾿ ὡς πᾶρ πᾶρὰ τοῦ φυλάσσω πεφύλακ ται φυλακτὸς, κỹ τέτακται τακ ϛ᾿ τὸ ϛ᾿ οὐκỹ τὸ ἄ τακ ϛ᾿ ατακ τῶ, οὕτω ϛ᾿ βέβακ ται βακ ϛ᾿. ϛ᾿ ῥῆμα ξ᾿ αὐτοῦ ἀβακτῶ, ἄσα τακ ϛ᾿ ἄτακτῶ. καὶ ἀφαιρέσει τοῦ τ, ἀβακῶ. ὃ τι καὶ τὸ

(marginalia)
Ἱπποκ᾽ς.

Abarms cimt.
Percote cimt.

Priapus Veneris et liber
F.

the partnership of Zacharias Kalliergis and Nikolaos Vlastos was dissolved. Kalliergis went to Padua for a short period and earned a living by copying manuscripts. In 1509 he returned to Venice and made a second attempt to establish a Greek press. He printed three works, one being the very first edition of the Ὡρολόγιον (1509).

We next find Kalliergis in Rome as a teacher at the newly established Greek Gymnasium founded by Pope Leo X. However, it was not long before he began printing again. He was the first to introduce Greek printing in the city of the Popes when in 1515 he brought out Pindar's Ὀλύμπια followed by the Εἰδύλλια of Theokritos (1516). It was also in Rome

that he brought out the first edition of another liturgical book, the Ὀκτώηχος (1520). Scholars now believe that Zacharias Kalliergis was the printer in charge of a series of editions brought out by the Greek Gymnasium Press and edited by Ianos (Janus) Laskaris (1445–1534) who was the director of the school.

The last publication to bear Kalliergis' name was the *Lexikon* of Guarino of Favera (1523). His activities can only be traced up to 1524 when he signed his name on a manuscript of that date. After this all trace of him is lost.

1962–The gift of Mr. and Mrs. Ward M. Canaday.

18. Manouel Philes, c.1275–c.1340. Στίχοι περὶ ζώων ἰδιότητος. 1565. Ms. on paper.

19. Eusebius Pamphili, Bishop of Caesaria. Ἐκκλησιαστικὴ ἱστορία. Lutetiae Parisiorum, Ex officina Roberti Stephani typographi Regii, Regiis typis, 1544.

The text of the Philes is a treatise in verse on various animals, birds, and fish, and was written by the Byzantine author Manouel Philes of Ephesos. The manuscript is from the hand of Angelos Vergikios who copied it in Paris in 1565. Angelos Vergikios (d. 1569) was from Crete and began his career as a scribe in Venice and Rome but in 1539 he moved to France at the invitation of Francis I and remained in his service as *escripvain en lectre grecque pour le Roy*. Besides his duties as a scribe for the king Vergikios also taught Greek to various well-known personages such as the son of Lazare de Baïf, Pierre de Ronsard, and Henri Estienne.

In 1539 Francis I, wishing to publish some of the manuscripts in the Royal collections in order to stimulate Greek studies in France, appointed Conrad Neobar Royal printer; however, Neobar died soon after and the task was taken over by Robert Estienne (Stephanus), who was appointed Royal Printer for Greek. A new font was planned for these publications, one based on the elegant handwriting of Angelos Vergikios. Vergikios' role in the design of the letters is often passed over and all the credit is given to Claude Garamond, the well-known founder who cut the punches and cast the type. The three sizes of type

produced by Garamond after the Vergikios hand have come to be known as *les grecs du roi* and became the most famous Greek type of the sixteenth century. It was imitated and copied widely all over Europe and its influence lasted for over two hundred years. It is now believed that the headpieces and decorative initials used by Estienne in the books printed with the *grecs du roi* (such as in the Eusebius shown here) and which were first attributed to Geoffroy Tory were actually derived from decorations found in manuscripts which were written by Angelos Vergikios. Vergikios had a son, Nikolaos, who was a friend of Ronsard and Baïf. There is also mention of a daughter who was an illuminator and who was supposed to have helped her father in his work.

The manuscript of Manouel Philes has a dedication to the Emperor Michael Palaiologos that appears at the beginning of the work. The whole manuscript is lavishly illuminated with one hundred and sixty miniatures of real and imaginary creatures which are divided into three sections: winged, terrestrial, and aquatic. At the end the manuscript gives the date and is signed Ἄγγελος.

1984–Philip Hofer Bequest.

Βοῦς.

Τάρανδος.

Περὶ ἐλάφου :~

Περὶ Ταράνδου :~

Περὶ Βοός :~

18

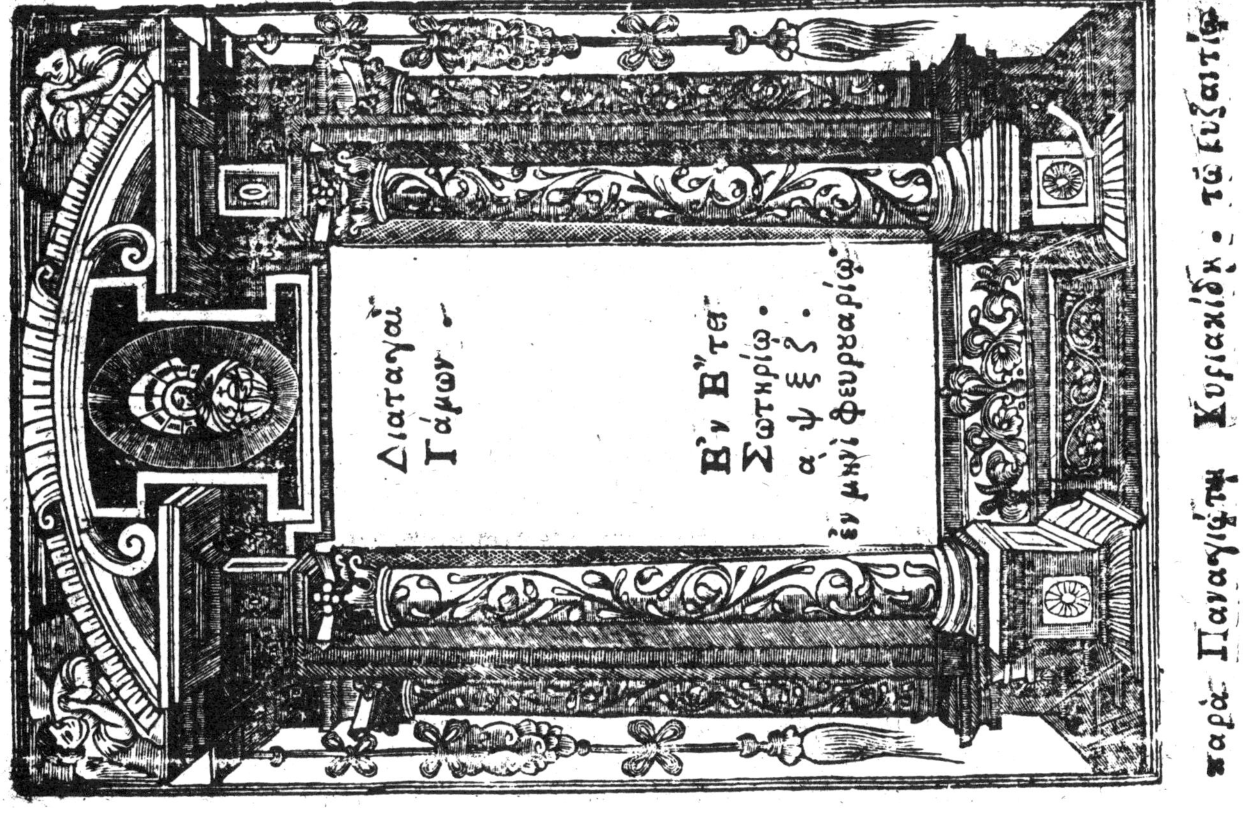

118

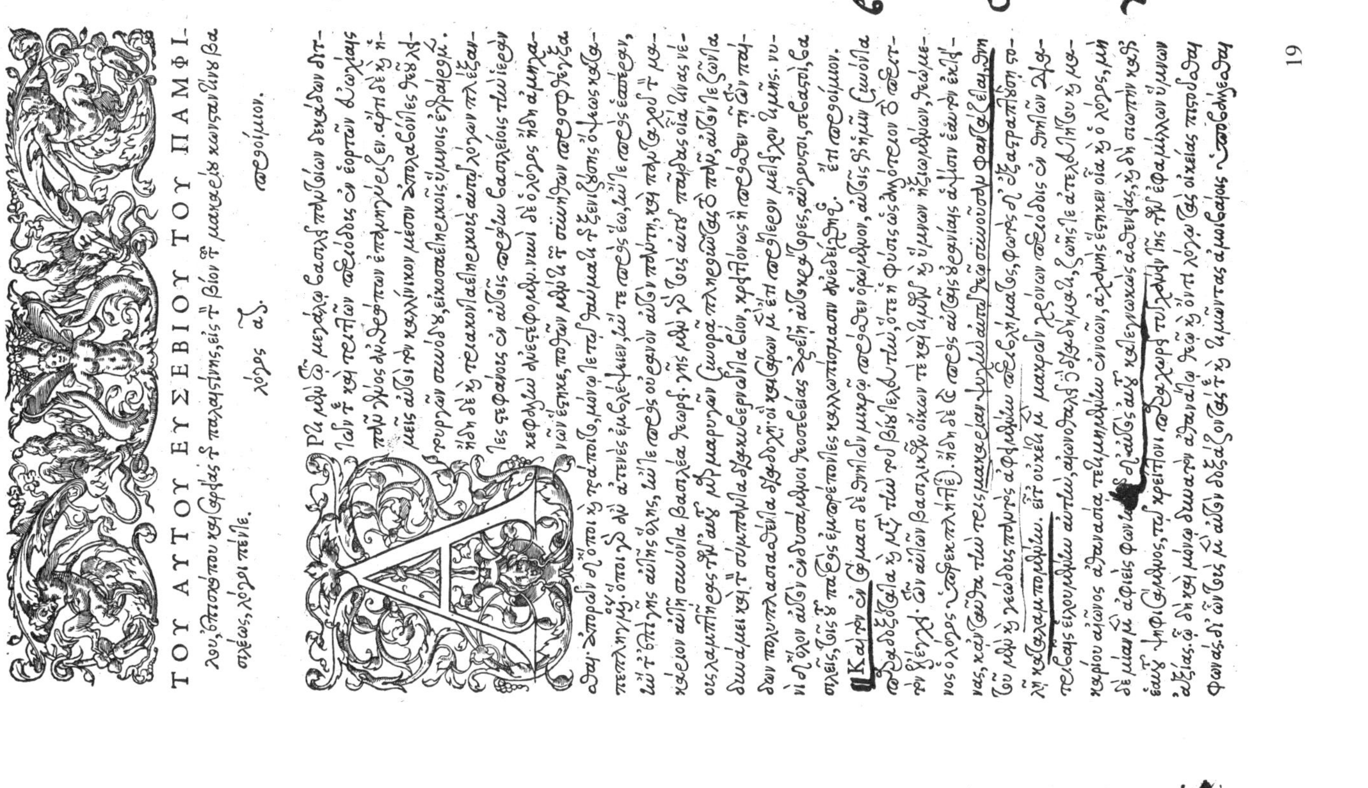

ΤΟΥ ΑΥΤΟΥ ΕΥΣΕΒΙΟΥ ΤΟΥ ΠΑΜΦΙ.

λου, ἱστορικῶν καὶ ἐγκωμίων τῆς παναγιωτάτης εἰς τ̄ βίον τ̄ μακαρίου κωνσταντίνου βα σιλέως, λόγος πέντε.

λόγος α΄.

19

15

Διαταγαὶ
Γάμων ·

Ἐν Β΄τῷ
Σωτηρίῳ ·
αφξζ.
ἐν μηνὶ Φευρραρίῳ·

παρὰ Παναγιώτῃ Κυριακίδῃ · τῷ Ευζαπι...

20

20. Christophoros Angelos, c. 1575–1638. *Πόνησις.* At Oxford, Printed by John Lichfeild and William Wrench printers to the famous Vniversitie, 1617.

The whole title in the English translation of the *Πόνησις* reads as follows: "Christopher Angell, a Grecian, who tasted of many stripes and torments inflicted by the Turkes for the faith which he had in Christ Iesus".

Christophoros Angelos was born in Gastouni in the Peloponnese and at an early age became a monk. In 1606 or 1607 he went to Athens to further his education. While studying there he was mistaken by the Turkish Governor of Athens for a Spanish spy. The reason for the confusion, according to Angelos, came from the fact that he was wearing the red habit of the Order of Saint Basil. He was arrested and thrown in jail. His trial took place on the eve of the Turkish religious feast of Bairam and the Turkish authorities demanded that Angelos embrace Islam in order to be set free. Angelos refused, was again thrown in jail, and was tortured.

In his book Angelos tells of his trials and tribulations in vivid terms. Finally, with the help of some friends he was able to escape from jail and left Athens behind him. He arrived in Yarmouth, England via Flanders and was lucky to have met in Yarmouth the bishop of Norwich who befriended him, gave him some money and sent him to study in Cambridge University. Angelos spent two years there at Trinity College. He later went to Oxford and continued his studies at Balliol College. After his studies, with the exception of some trips to London and elsewhere in England, Angelos taught beginning Greek to the younger students at Balliol.

Angelos also wrote and published other works in Greek and in English translation, the best known of which was *On the Condition of Life in Which the Greeks now Live* (1625). The work first came out in Greek in 1624 and was later translated into Latin in 1655 and into German in 1664. Angelos died in Oxford in 1638 at the age of sixty-four and was buried in the churchyard of Saint Ebbe. Among the Greeks who studied at Balliol in the seventeenth century were Metrophanes Kritopoulos from Veroia in Macedonia, who later became Patriarch of Alexandria, and Nathanael Konopios, who was credited with having introduced the drinking of coffee at Oxford.

1967–Gift of Christian A. Zabriskie in memory of Edward Powis Jones

ΙΧΝΟΓΡΑΦΙΑ ΤΗΣ ΠΟΤΕ ΚΩΝΣΤΑΝΤΙΝΟΥΠΟΛΕΩΣ.

2 Τὸ μακρὺ γεφύριον. 3 Καταφύγιον τῶν καραβίων τὸ ὀνομαζόμενον Κανδεκοιλίον. 4 Λιμὴν τȣ βασιλικȣ παλατίȣ. 5 Ἡ Ὀδηγήτρια. 6 Ὁ ἅγιος Γεώργιος τῶν Μαγγανῶν. 7 Ἀνατολή. 8 Ὁ ἅγιος Δημήτριος. 9 Γȣδαίας πύλη. 10 Ὁ ψαραδα πύλη. 11 Μεσαία πύλη. 12 Πύλη Χεῖνε. 13 Ἐ'δὰ ἐκτυπȣσαν οἱ Τȣρκοι ὄντα τὰ Τείχη ἀδυνατώτερα. 14 Ὁ ἅγιος Γωάννης τῶν Στȣδίων. 15 Πύλη ἀρχαιοτάτη ἡ ἐπωνομαζομένη ὡραία. 16 Τῶν ἁγίων Ἀποστόλων ναός. 17 Ἡ ἁγία Σοφία.

21. Georgios Phrantzes, fl. 15th. cent. παρὰ Μαρκίδ. Πούλιου 1796.

Χρονικόν. Ἐν Βιέννῃ τῆς Ἀουστρίας,

This work of Georgios Phrantzes chronicles the events of the last dynasty of Byzantium, the Palaiologan. It also describes the Siege and Fall of Constantinople on May 29, 1453. Phrantzes, who was a diplomat in the Palaiologan court and was himself captured by the Turks, was later set free. He visited Italy, Venice, and Rome. His chronicle stops in the year 1476. This is the first edition of the Phrantzes chronicle in Greek. A Latin translation was first published by Jacob Pontanus as an appendix in his edition of Theophylactus Simocatta in 1604.

The publishers of the work were the brothers Poublios and Georgios Markides Pouliou from Siatista in Macedonia who were very active in Vienna as publishers and who also brought out a newspaper *Ἐφημερίς* between 1790 and 1798. This was the second Greek newspaper published in Vienna. The first was that of Georgios Ventotes, copies of which do not survive today. The articles in the newspaper were to be written in the "simple romaic" (*ἀπλῆν*

ῥωμαϊκὴν γλῶσσαν), as it was announced in the prospectus of the newspaper. The *Ἐφημερίς* became the vehicle for the dissemination to the Greek speaking world under Turkish domination of the new ideas of liberalism and democracy that prevailed in Europe. The brothers Markides Pouliou printed their newspaper at the press of Joseph Baumeister. When Baumeister was appointed tutor to the royal princes in 1792 he turned over the direction of his printing establishment to the brothers, who during their tenure as overseers of the press printed a good number of Greek books.

Because of the close association between Regas Velestinles with the brothers Markides Pouliou, after Regas' arrest and execution both the newspaper and the Baumeister-Pouliou press were shut down by the Austrian authorities and the brothers Markides Pouliou were expelled from Austria.

1977 – Duplicate Fund.

Ἀπόκοπον τὰ μπεργαδῆ,
Ρήμα λογιότατη,
Τὴν ἔχουσιν οἱ φρόνιμοι,
Πολλὰ ποθεινοτάτη.

Μίαν Ἀποκόπου ἐνύσταξα,
Νὰ κοιμηθῶ ἐθυμήθην,
Ἤθεκα τὸ κρεββάτιωμου,
Κ' ὕπνον ὑπνοκοιμήθην.
Ἐφάνημου κ' ἔτρεχα,
Εἰς λιβάδιν ὡραιωμένον,
Φαρὶν ἐκαβαλίκευγα,
Σελλοχαλινωμένον.
Κ' εἶχα τὴν ζώσημου σπαθὶν,
Στὸ χέριμου κοντάριν,
Σωσμένος ἤμουν ἄρματα,
Σαγίτες καὶ δοξάριν.
Κ' ἐφάνημου ὁ κίδιοχνα,
Μὲ θράσος ἰλαφίνα,
Ὧρες ἐκοντοσίκετον,
καὶ ὧρες μὲ βίαν ἐκίνα.
Προσωὸν τὰ τρέχειν ἤρχησα,
Τάχα νὰ βάλω χέρα,
Ἔτρεχα ὥστε καὶ τζάκισε,
Τὸ σαύρωμα ἡμέρα.
Κ' ἐξαυτὺς ἀπὸ τὰ μάτιαμου,
Ἐχάθηκεν τὸ λαφὶν,
καὶ πῶς καὶ ποτὲ χάθηκεν,
Ἐξαπορῶ τὸ γράφειν.
Λοιπὸν τὸ τρέχειν ὄπαυσαν,
Οὕτως καὶ τὸ σπουδάζειν,
καὶ τὸ ξετρίχειν τ' ἀπίασον,
καὶ τὸ φαρὶν κολάζειν.
Καὶ ἀγάλιγαλι ἐπήγαινα,
Σιγὰ σιγὰ περπάτουν,
Τὸν κόσμον ἐξενίζουμου,
Τ' ἄνθη καὶ τὰ καλάτου.
Καὶ πρὸς τὴν δήμην ἔσωσα,
Στὰ λιβαδίου τὴν μέσην,
Κ' ηὗρα δέντρον ἐξαίρετον,
καὶ ὠρέχθην τὰ πεζεύσειν.
Ἐπίασα εἰς τὸ δέντρον,
Κ' ἔδεσα τ' ἀλογόνμου,
καὶ τ' ἄρματα ἐξεζώσηκα,
Θετώτα τὸ πλαρύνμου.
Ὁ τόπος ὁποῦ ἐπίασα,
Λίγω ἐκεῖ ὁποῦ ἰσάθην,
Ἤτον τὸ λιβαδίου ὀφαλλὸς,
Κ' ἦτον γεμάτος τ' ἄνθη.

Τὸ δένδρον ἦτον τρυφερὸν,
Κ' εἶλεν πυκνὰ τὰ φύλλα,
Εἶχεν καὶ σύγκαρπον ἀδὸν,
καὶ μυριστικὰ μῆλα.
Καὶ μυριαρίθμητα πουλία,
Στὸν δενδρὸν φωλεμένα,
Κατὰ τὴν φύσιν καὶ σκοπὸν,
Ἐλάλειν τὸ καθ' ἕνα.
Καὶ ἀπὸ τὰ κάλλη τὰ δενδροῦ,
τὴν ἡδονὴν τὰ τόπου,
καὶ τὴν πλείων τὴν μελωδίαν,
καὶ ὁλημερνοῦ τὰ σόπου.
Ὡς ἀπὸ βίας ἠκούμπησα,
τὸ πεῖ ἀπασαίνω,
καὶ ἐσοχάζομην τὸ δεντρὸν,
Εἰς τὴν κορφὴν ἀπάνω.
Καὶ ἐφάνειμε εἶδα ἐκάθετον,
Μελίσσιν φωλεμένον,
Κ' εἶχε τὸ μέλι σύγκερον,
Πολλὰ καὶ σωσμένον.
Εὐθὺς τ' ἀνέβην ὥρμησα,
καὶ τὴν τροφὴν ὠρέχθην,
καὶ τὸ μελίσσιν μὲ θυμὸν,
Ἀπὸ μακρὰ μ' ἐδέχθην.
Λοιπὸν ἀνέβην τὸν δενδρόν,
Μὲ βίαν πολλὴν καὶ κόπον,
καὶ ὁποῦ ἰβλεπα τὴν μέλισσαν,
Ἐκάθιζα τὸν τόπον.
Ἡ πλωτ' ἐπίασα ἐκτὸ κεὶν,
Κ' ἔφαγ' ἀπὸ τὸ μέλι,
κ' ἐπέμου μέσα ὁ λογισμὸς,
Δὸς τῆς ψυχῆς τὸ θέλει.
Ἔτρωγα οὐκ ἐχόρτενα,
Ἤρπουν καὶ πάντα ἐπείνουν,
καὶ ὡς πεινασμένος εἰς τὸ φαΐν,
Ὕστερα παλ' ἐκείνουν,
Κ' ἡ μέλισσα οὐκ ἔπαυεν,
Πάντα νὰ μὲ δοξάζει,
καὶ τὸ δενδρὸν ἀρχήνησεν,
Ὡς οἶδα νὰ σαλάθη.
Νὰ συχνοτρέμη νὰ χαλᾷ,
Νὰ δείχνη κάτω νάρθη,
κ' ἐγὼ τὸ φαΐν ἔσκοτωσα,
καὶ ἀπὸ τὰ φόβου ἐπάρθην.
Καὶ ἐσιχαζόμην τὸ δενδρὸν,
Τοὺς κλώνουςτου τριγύρου,
καὶ πάλιν μέσα τὸ βλέπω,
Τὶς πόσειν ἐσωτήρου.
Καὶ δύο μ' ὀφάνιν ποντικοὶ,
τὸ δένδρον ἐγύριζαν,
Ἄσπρος δ' μαῦρος μὲ σπουδὴν,
τὰ ἐγλύφασιν τὴν ρίζαν.

Εἰς

Vernacular Texts

The first text in modern Greek to appear in print was the *Apokopos* of Bergadis (1519) written at the beginning of the fifteenth century. Other vernacular texts and translations into modern Greek followed soon after, so that by the middle of the sixteenth century a good number of vernacular texts were published. Some of these proved so popular that they came out in several editions during the sixteenth century and continued to be in use well into the nineteenth century.

The preponderance of modern Greek texts printed during this period were in rhyme. Besides works of contemporary authors like Antonios Achelis, Markos Depharanas, Gioustos Glykys, Iakovos Trivolis and Tzanes Ventramos, there were a number of translations from ancient into modern Greek and also from Italian. Among the classics were Homer's *Iliad*, the *Batrachomyomachia*, Aesop's *Fables*, and Plutarch's *Peri paidon agoges*. From Italian there was Boccaccio's *Teseide* and the *Fior di virtù*. By far the most popular were the rhymed versions of such stories as that of Apollonius of Tyre, the Alexander the Great romance, the story of Belisarios and the story of Imberios.

During the second half of the sixteenth century some clerics began to use modern Greek to write their sermons. The most successful and popular of these were the sermons of Damaskenos Stoudites. His sermons, popularly known as *Thesauros*, came out in numerous editions in the sixteenth century and continued to be published throughout the *Tourkokratia*. The same holds true for the work of Emmanouel Glyzounis' arithmetic, the *Logariastike*, which was used extensively as one of the few practical compendiums written during this period. A grammar of the modern Greek language was written in the 1550's by Nikolaos Sophianos but it remained in manuscript form until the nineteenth century when it was published by Émile Legrand.

More contemporary literary works appeared in print in the seventeenth and eighteenth centuries such as Chortatses' *Erophile* (1637), the anonymously written *Voskopoula* (1638), Bouniales' *Diegeses* (1681), the *Sacrifice of Abraham* (1691), and Kornaros' *Erotokritos*, all fine examples of Cretan literature. To these works were added the works of ecclesiastics who continued to write in modern Greek such as the Cretan monk Agapios Landos, whose *Hamartolon soteria* was first printed in 1641 and continued to appear up to our times. In 1631 the *Vivlion historikon* of pseudo-Dorotheos, bishop of Monemvasia, made its first appearance. This chronicle is made up of various Byzantine, post-Byzantine and other chronicles beginning with the creation of the world up to the end of the sixteenth century. The work became very popular and went through several editions in the seventeenth century. It continued to be reprinted until 1814.

22. [Bergadis].   Ἀπόκοπος. Ἐνετίησιν, παρὰ Ὀρσίνῳ Ἀλβρίτζῃ 1667

The Ἀπόκοπος was the first modern Greek text to be printed. The chapbooks or *rimades* printed in the sixteenth century were aimed at a broader public and were not addressed to the intellectual élite, who were more involved with the classical Greek texts that were published in abundance in Italy and elsewhere in Europe at this time. Since these *phyllades* were not exactly collector's items a good percentage of them have been lost to us. Only last year was the first edition of the Ἀπόκοπος, Venice, 1509, located and identified. Fortunately, the Ἀπόκοπος survived in several editions from the sixteenth through the nineteenth centuries. It has also survived in two manuscripts, one of which is a copy of the printed edition.

Almost nothing is known about Bergadis, the author

of the Ἀπόκοπος. The name Bergadis is thought to be a hellenized version of the Venetian name Bragadin. Members of this family had settled in Rethymnon, Crete. The Bergadis family can be traced in Crete from 1311. Scholars agree that the work was written toward the end of the fifteenth century. The central theme of the *Apokopos* is that life is ephemeral. The plot centers on the poet's descent to Hades as experienced in a dream. While there, he meets and talks with two young men who want to know what is happening above and especially if their loved ones remember them. The poet's response is that the only ones who have not forgotten them are their mothers. Despite the somber story of the poem, the work is actually a celebration of life and is considered to be one of the most poetic works of this period. It was extremely popular among the Greek people for centuries and parts of it survive today in the form of *moirologia*, especially in Crete.

1970–Harry Knowles Messenger and Ada Messenger Fund and the Friends of the Harvard College Library.

23. Homer. Ἰλιάς, μεταβληθεῖσα εἰς κοινὴν γλῶσσαν . . . παρὰ Νικολάου τοῦ Λουκάνου. Venetia, per Maestro Stefano da Sabio . . . ad instantia di miser Damiano di Santa Maria da Spici 1526.

The Loukanis paraphrase of Homer's Iliad was the first translation into a vernacular language to be printed, and it was fitting that the language was modern Greek. The full title of the Iliad reads thus as translated by Francis R. Walton: "The Iliad of Homer, transformed long ago into the common tongue and now corrected, abridged, and arranged book by book, as in the Homeric text, by Nikolaos Loukanis. It is a very useful book and one that will delight those who read it. And since many difficult, or Homeric, words occur in it, a list has been provided where you will find these Homeric words simply explained. Accept therefore this book so that you may come to know the manifold achievements of Homer."

The translation is based on an earlier paraphrase made by Konstantinos Hermoniakos, who lived under the Despot of Epirus, Ioannes Komnenos Angelos Doukas (1323–1335). Loukanis' version follows the Byzantine Homeric tradition of adding at the end of the Iliad the story of the Fall of Troy which is taken from the Byzantine Achilleid.

Nikolaos Loukanis of Zakynthos was one of the first students to attend the Greek school (Gymnasium) founded by the Medici Pope Leo X in Rome in 1514 and directed by Ianos (Janus) Laskaris. Other than this nothing is known about Nikolaos Loukanis.

Printed in red below the title is a mark, a marten (in Greek κουνάδι) within a shield, which is the publisher's device of Andreas Kounadis. Andreas Kounadis of Patras, a well-to-do businessman residing in Venice, had founded in 1521 or perhaps as early as 1519, a publishing firm in order to print the liturgical books of the Orthodox Church and also a series of texts in modern Greek for wider circulation. In order to achieve this he engaged the services of the printers, the brothers Nicolini da Sabio, who had experience in the printing of Greek texts and who at the time had been working for Andrea Torresani, the partner and father-in-law of Aldus Manutius. Andreas Kounadis died prematurely at the end of 1522 but the firm continued to operate until 1553 under the leadership of Kounadis' father-in-law, Damiano di Santa Maria from Spic in Illyria, concentrating exclusively on the publication of liturgical and modern Greek texts. The mark of Andreas Kounadis came to symbolize Greek books for Greek readers. The publisher of modern Greek texts and liturgical books, Giacomo Leoncini, purchased the mark and printing types of the Kounadis firm and in 1560 launched his own firm, displaying the Kounadis mark along with his own. Thereafter the mark of Kounadis was used by a succession of printers making its last appearance on the titlepage of a modern Greek edition of the Alexander the Great romance in 1600.

The modern Greek Iliad is illustrated with one hundred and thirty-eight woodcuts (five of them repeats) which were later used to illustrate other modern Greek texts printed by the firm, among them editions of the Alexander the Great romance, of the Imberios romance, and others. The wooducts were fashioned in the Venetian style of the period, a fact which scandalized classical scholars of the nineteenth century who found them crude and inappropriate for a poem such as the Iliad. The Loukanis Iliad, perhaps because of its length, was not reprinted in the sixteenth century but was printed again in 1603 and in 1640.

1952–Duplicate Fund.

ἔρριψ᾽ οἷα χρυσὸν νέφος,   ἀπὸ πάνω εἰς τὰ νότους·
ἵνα μὴ τινὰς τοὺς ἴδῃ,   οὕτως ἥσυχος κοιμᾶται·
ὁ πατὴρ ὁ ζωὰς τῶν πάντων,   ἐκ τῇ ὕπνου καὶ ἀγάπης·
δαμασθεὶς ὁ ἄθλιος τότε,   καὶ ἐκράτει εἰς ταὶς ἀγκάλαις·
τὴν ὡραίαν του τὴν Ἥραν.

καὶ αὐτίκα μὲν ὁ ὕπνος,   εἰς τὰς νήσους τῶν ἀρχαίων·
ὥσπερ ἄγγελος ὑπάγει,   εἰς αὐτὸν τὸν ποσειδῶνα·
καὶ σταθεὶς πλησίον τούτου,   εἶπε πρὸς αὐτὸν τοιαῦτα·
Ποσειδῶν μὲ πρὸ θυμίαν,   νῦν βοήθα τῷ ἀργείοις·
δὸς τοὺς καὶ μεγάλην δόξαν, τὸν βραχὺν τὸν καιρὸν τῆτον·
ἕως ποῦ ὁ ζωὰς κοιμᾶται,   ἐπειδὴ ἐγὼ εἰς τὸν τῆτον·
ἔρριψα μεγάλον ὕπνον,   ἡ δὲ ἥρα ἡ γυνή του·
τὸν ἐγέλασε σιὼ κλίνω,   οὕτως ἔλεξεν ὁ ὕπνος·
καὶ ἀπῆλθε τοὺς ἀνθρώπους, ἵνα ἅπαντας ὑπνώσει·
κ᾽ ἔποισε τὸν ποσειδῶνα,   τὸν αὐθέντην τῆς θαλάσσης·

23

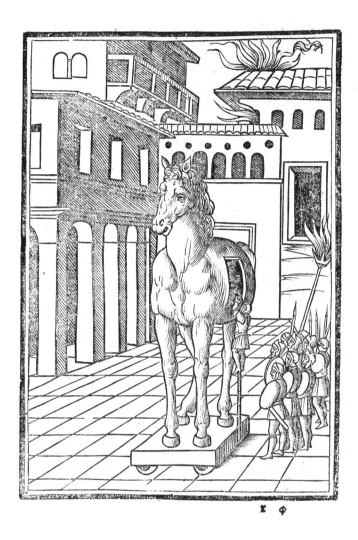

𝕩 φ

23

24. Ἄνθος τῶν χαρίτων.   Venezia, per Francesco Andreola 1830.

From its very first edition in 1529 the Ἄνθος τῶν χαρίτων was a very popular chapbook with the Greek people. It was the first prose work of this genre to be printed. Before this, all the other chapbooks were in verse. The Ἄνθος τῶν χαρίτων is a translation of the Italian *Fior di virtù*, a work which had great success not only in Italy but throughout Europe and was even translated into Arabic and Armenian. The authorship of the *Fior di virtù* is not clear. It was perhaps written by Tommaso Gozzadini a little before 1323. The Italian version had gone through sixty-six editions in the fifteenth century alone.

The modern Greek translation was first printed in 1529. Five editions survive from the sixteenth century,

six in the seventeenth, ten in the eighteenth and twelve in the first half of the nineteenth century. More editions have probably disappeared or are as yet unrecorded. It has also survived in six manuscripts, three of which antedate the printed Greek editions. Not all the editions of the work have remained faithful to the original version of 1529. In the seventeenth century, beginning with the 1603 edition, the work was revised. Beginning with the 1755 edition the work was completely redone, new material was inserted, and the title was changed to Νέον ἄνθος χαρίτων. Some editions give the Italian and Greek in parallel columns. The book was often used as a reader for those learning either Greek or Italian. Beginning with

the 1812 edition the title returned to the original style, although the various changes which had occurred through the years remained.

The Ἄνθος χαρίτων is an anthology that enumerates and describes the various virtues and corresponding vices. Each is compared to an animal or a bird which seems to have similar characteristics in shape or behavior. The translator of the Greek version is not known. The work is written in the modern Greek language of the period. There are indications in the sources that the work was used as a schoolbook during the *Tourkokratia*.

1887 – Bequest of Professor E. A. Sophocles.

25. Aesop. *Μῦθοι.* Ἐνετίησι, Ἐν τῇ Σαληκάτῃ, ἀναλώμασι τῆς Ἱερᾶς τῶν φίλων Ξυνωρίδος 1644

This modern Greek edition of Aesop's fables was printed by a little known press that was active for only four years (1643–1646). During this period the press produced some twenty Greek books, most of them for ecclesiastical or instructional purposes. The press originally belonged to the heirs of Altobello Salicato and it appears that it was bought and financed by members of the Greek community of Venice, who in 1642 petitioned for permission to print certain works through the intermediary of the Orthodox archbishop of Venice (officially the Archbishop of Philadelphia), Athanasios Valerianos. The principal backer of this enterprise was the wealthy Angelos Benizelos.

The book is illustrated with fifty-eight woodcuts

(four of them are repetitions) which were originally designed by Giovanni Mario Verdizotti (1525–1600) for his *Cento favole morali* (Venice, 1570). Verdizotti was a pupil and friend of Titian and some of the woodcuts are attributed to Titian himself. The Verdizotti work used one hundred woodcuts that were still in use as late as 1661 when the *Cento favole*

morali were reprinted. This borrowing of woodcuts and their use to print works of different subject matter was a very common practice among the printers of the Renaissance.

1984 – Philip Hofer Bequest.

26. [Markos Depharanas] fl. 1543–1569. Ἱστορία τῆς Σωσάννης. Ἐνετίησιν, παρὰ Ὀρσίνῳ Ἀλβρίτζῃ, 1667.

The name of the poet does not appear on the titlepage in any of the editions of this story of Susanna, but instead is given in the initial letters of the first twenty-five distichs of the work. It is explained at the very end of the poem, in the last distich, that the name of the author can be found at the beginning. Depharanas has used a similar technique in another of his works printed in 1543, the Λόγοι διδακτικοὶ τοῦ πατρὸς πρὸς τὸν υἱόν, where in the last six verse lines of the text he informs the reader that he came from the Ionian Island of Zakynthos and that he had later moved to Venice. Beyond these few facts almost nothing is known about the author.

Depharanas belongs to a group of Ionian Island writers who were active between 1520 and 1570 and who wrote their works in modern Greek. Among them are Ioannikios Kartanos, who wrote the first modern Greek translation of the stories of the Bible, Iakovos Trivolis, Alexios Rhartouros, and Nikolaos Sophianos, all of Corfu. The latter made the first modern Greek translation of Plutarch and also wrote an admirable grammar of the modern Greek language which remained in manuscript form until the end of the nineteenth century. Besides Depharanas, the island of Zakynthos produced Nikolaos Loukanis, the first translator of the Iliad, and Demetrios Zenos, the first editor and adapter of many modern Greek texts that were printed in Venice during the first half of the sixteenth century.

The earliest Greek edition of the Susanna story in existence today is the one published in Venice by Giacomo Leoncini in 1569. This edition survived in only one copy, that which belonged to Martinus Crusius (1526–1607). The story of Susanna is based on the version in the Old Testament and although there is a late fourteenth century Greek manuscript of the poem the story as told by Markos Depharanas is most probably based on an Italian prototype. The story was very popular throughout Europe during the sixteenth century. None of the other Greek sixteenth century

editions have come down to us although we know of their existence from other sources. A number of editions from the seventeenth, eighteenth and nineteenth centuries exist today.

1966 – Patrick Grant II Fund (HC 1908).

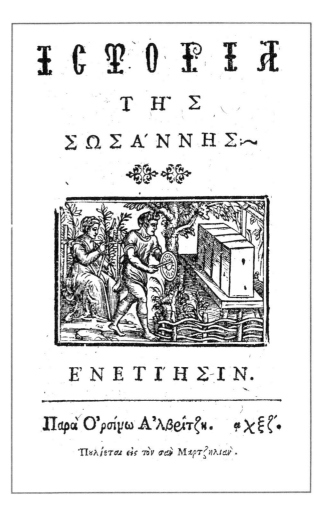

26

27. Georgios Chortatses, c. 1545–1610. Τραγωδία, ὀνομαζομένη Ἐρωφίλη. Ἐνετίησιν, παρὰ Δημητρίῳ Θεοδοσίου τῷ ἐξ Ἰωαννίνων 1772.

Georgios Chortatses was one of the most important literary figures of the Cretan Renaissance (1570–1669). This important period in Cretan culture also produced Domenikos Theotokopoulos (El Greco) and Kyrillos Loukaris, successively Patriarch of Alexandria and Constantinople, and one of the most enlightened prelates of the Orthodox Church. It is significant that modern Greek literature which had its beginnings already in the fifteenth century, reached its first high point in Crete, which did not fall to the Turks until 1669. It later continued and flourished in another part of Greece, one that never experienced the Turkish Occupation, the Ionian Islands.

Georgios Chortatses was born in Rethymnon. His family belonged to the nobility of the island and he must have spent some years in Italy for he was well-educated and well-versed in Italian literature. His tragedy Ἐρωφίλη was first published in 1637, after the death of its author. It was modelled after an Italian work, the *Orbecche* of Giovanni Battista Giraldi, which was performed for the first time in Ferrara in 1541 and was first published in 1561. However, Chortatses' work is not a translation of the *Orbecche* and neither is it a mere reworking of the story; it is an original piece of work. Ἐρωφίλη is the oldest and most important work of the Cretan theater. Like all the other works of this period, it was written in the spoken Cretan dialect of its time. According to the literary historian Linos Politis, perhaps never before was the demotic language written with such clarity and consistency in modern Greek literature.

Chortatses' other plays include Πανώρια, a pastoral drama also known as Γύπαρις, and Κατζοῦρμπος, a comedy. The 1772 edition above, is from the press of Demetrios Theodosiou, originally from Ioannina, who operated one of the three important Greek publishing firms in Venice in the eighteenth century. The press of Demetrios and Panos Theodosiou was active between 1755 and 1824.

1974 – Purchased with the Salisbury Fund.

28. Marinos Tzanes Bouniales, d.c. 1686. Διήγησις διὰ στίχων τοῦ δεινοῦ πολέμου τοῦ ἐν τῇ νήσῳ Κρήτης λεγομένου. Ἐνετίησιν, παρὰ Ἀνδρέᾳ τῷ Ἰουλιανῷ 1681.

This long poem chronicles the Fall of Crete to the Turks in 1669. It is a detailed, chronological account of the war from the time the Turks landed in Crete in 1645 up until the very end. The author used his own experiences of the war and those he learned from others when they were all refugees in the Ionian Islands. However, for some of the events he also used as a point of reference the work of a Venetian author, Andrea Valiero, *La guerra di Candia* and the work of Anthimos Diakrouses of Cephalonia. Although the work is not very skilfully written as a piece of poetic expression, the passion and fervent tone of the writer endow it with interest.

Marinos Tzanes Bouniales was from a noble family of Rethymnon. He was the brother of Emmanuel Tzanes Bouniales who was a priest of San Giorgio dei Greci in Venice and who was himself a poet and hagiographer. Marinos and his brothers lived in Rethymnon until it fell to the Turks. From there they went to Corfu and later to Venice, where his work was printed in 1681. Marinos Tzanes Bouniales also wrote another poem entitled Κατάνυξις ὠφέλιμος διὰ κάθε Χριστιανόν, which was printed in Venice in 1684.

1970 – Harry Knowles Messenger and Ada Messenger Fund and the Friends of the Harvard College Library.

29. Πανουργίαι ὑψηλόται Μπερτόλδου. Ἐν Βενετίᾳ παρὰ Νικολάῳ Γλυκεῖ, 1818.

The story of Bertoldo was written by Giulio Cesare Croce (1550–1609) and was translated from the Italian into modern Greek sometime before its first edition in 1646, put out by the Italian printer of Greek works Giannantonio Giuliani. The translator is not known but he has rendered the work in a very good and flowing demotic.

The printer of the first edition of Bertoldo,

5

ΕΥΜΟΡΦΙΑΙ
ΤΟΥ
ΜΠΕΡΤΟΛΔΟΥ

Ο Μισὲρ ΜΠΕΡΤΟΛΔΟΣ ἤτον μικρο῾σρο῾σ῾ωπος, χον-
῾σοκέφαλος, ὁλοςρόγγυλος ὡς φοῦσκα, τὸ μέ-
τωπόν τε ζαρωμςίον, τὰ μάτιά του κόκκινα ὡς φω-
τία, τὰ φρύδιά τε μακρὰ, κỳ ἄζεια ὡς γκρκνό῾ϝιχες,
τὰ αὐτιά τε γαϊδάρινα, μεγαλόςομος, ςραβόςομος,
μὲ τὰ χείλη κρεμασμέςα κάτω ὡς τȣ ἀλόγȣ, τὰ
γςϝειά τε πυκνὰ, κỳ πο῎λὰ ὑποκάτω εἰς τὸ πηγȣν῀ί
τε, κỳ ἔπȣ῍δταν ὡς ἐκεῖνα τȣ Τράγȣ, ἡ μήπη τε ςρα-
βὴ, κỳ σηκωμένη ἐπάϝω, μὲ ταῖς ῾ϝύπαις πλατείαις·
τὰ δόντιά τε ἔζω ὡς τ῏ȣ Κάπρων, μὲ τεία, ἡ πέσ-
σα-
Α 3

29

Giannantonio Giuliani, was one of the few printers of his time who printed modern Greek texts of literary merit. He is credited with bringing out not only the first edition of the above work which became very successful with the Greek reading public, but also the first edition of Georgios Chortatses' Ἐρωφίλη (1637), the Βασιλεὺς Ῥοδολίνος of I. A. Troilos (1647), and many other works.

It is interesting to note that the ribald stories of Bertoldo offended the sensibilities of some Orthodox churchmen and the work was included among a number of other popular books that were considered immoral and indecent by Nikodemos Hagioreites (1749–1809), who condemned them as heretical along with the Ἐρωτόκριτος of V. Kornaros, the Σπανός, and the Βοσκοπούλα among others.

Bertoldo was printed regularly by the Venetian printers of Greek between 1646 and 1847.

1986–Cornelius Conway Felton Fund. The bequest of Emma F. Cary.

30. Vintzentzos Kornaros, fl. 17th cent. Ἐρωτόκριτος. Ἐν Βενετίᾳ, Ἐκ τῆς ἑλληνικῆς τυπογραφίας Νικολάου Γλυκῆ 1847.

Vintzentzos Kornaros from Sitia in Crete was the most important writer of the Cretan Renaissance (1570–1669). His Ἐρωτόκριτος a long poem of 10,052 verses can be better described as a novel written in verse which tells the love story of its protagonists Erotokritos and Aretousa.

Very little is known about Kornaros. Some scholars thought that he might have belonged to the Venetian Corner family, which had various branches living in Crete, but this view was rejected because the Venetian noble families of Crete kept themselves apart from the life and culture of Crete and none of them could have written a work so imbued with Greek popular culture. There were other Kornaroi in Crete, families that the author could have belonged to who had no connection with the Corner branch of Venice. However, to date no concrete evidence has been found to tell us about the author other than his name and place of birth, which are given in the epilogue of the work.

Scholars place the date of his birth at the beginning of the seventeenth century and the *Erotokritos* was written before the Fall of Crete to the Turks in 1669. The work has been influenced by Western models, especially by the French medieval romance of *Paris et Vienne* of Pierre de la Cypède. Despite the influence of *Paris et Vienne* the work is intensely Greek and is considered a classic example of modern Greek literature. Scholars have speculated that Kornaros wrote the *Erotokritos* between 1640 and 1660. The work was published posthumously in Venice in 1713; however, it was popular long before its publication, which attests that it had circulated in manuscript form. It has come down to us in several editions and in one manuscript now at the British Library. The poet George Seferis (1900–1971) in an essay on the *Erotokritos* describes how when he was growing up in Smyrna he bought a popular edition of the work from the itinerant peddler who used to pass by his house every day selling books and other wares.

1858–By exchange with the University of Athens, Greece.

Πρὸς τὸν ὑψηλότατον, Εὐσεβέςατον, καὶ Σοφώτατον Αὐθέντίω, καὶ Ἡγεμόνα
πάσης Οὐγγροβλαχίας, Κύριον, Κύριον, Ἰωάννω Νικόλαον
Ἀλέξανδρα Βοεβόδαν.

Ἤνεγκε βρῶσιν Ἠλία πάλαι Κόραξ,
Τῆς γῆς νοσούσης αὐχμὸν ἠδ᾽ ἀνομβρίαν.
Σταυρὰ δὲ νῦ τρόπαιον ἐν ῥάμφει φέρων,
Κάρηνα κοσμεῖ Κοιράνων τῶν Δακίης.
Ἐν οἷς χοραρχῶν Νικόλαος νῦ, πέλει
Ἴνδαλμα λαμπρὸν ἀγεςάτων τρόπων.
Σοφῶς κρατῶν οἴακας Οὐγγροβλαχίης,
Ὅπλον κραταιὸν Σταυρὸν ἠμφιεσμένος,
Πίςιν παρεδρὸν, καὶ δίκω κεκτημένος.
Βοὸς καρα δὲ δεικνύει κερασφόρα.
Ὀρθῶς ἰθῦαι καὶ θρόνον Μολδαβίης,
Ὃν Χριςὲ σώζοις Σταυρικῇ παντουχία.

Τῆς ὑμετέρας Θεοφρουρήτω Ὑψηλότητος
ἐλάχιςος δ᾽ἄλος Ἰωάννης Ποςελ:

The Greek Enlightenment and Its Antecedents

The Greek Enlightenment (1750–1830) was preceded by two periods, one of which overlaps with the first phase of the Greek Enlightenment. In the first period, that of Religious Humanism (1600–1669) there was a renaissance of philosophical studies and the beginning of the study of the Greek classics. The major exponents of this new beginning were the Patriarch Kyrillos Loukaris (1572–1638) and the Aristotelian philosopher Theophilos Korydalleus (1560–1645). It was followed by the Age of the Phanariots (1670–1770), a period that is characterized by a thirst for education and a turn toward the ideas of the West, especially France. The Phanariots, a class of wealthy Greek merchants, lived in the Fanar section of Constantinople near the Patriarchate which had been moved there in 1601. Because of their education and knowledge of foreign languages, the Phanariots held important positions in the Turkish government such as Grand Dragoman, i.e. Minister of Foreign Affairs. From 1661 to 1821 this post of Grand Dragoman was held by the Phanariots. Other high positions which became the preserve of the Phanariots were Dragoman of the Fleet and governors or Voivode of Moldavia and Wallachia.

The most important Phanariot family was that of the Mavrokordatos. Alexandros Mavrokordatos, the Exaporite (1636–1709) was Grand Dragoman to the Sultan, an educator and an author of note with several works to his credit. His son Nikolaos (1680–1730) was the first Phanariot to become Voivode of Moldavia in 1709. In c. 1718 he wrote φιλοθέου πάρεργα which was published anonymously in 1800. It is a series of conversations of worldly wisdom in the form of a novel. Nikolaos Mavrokordatos also translated the work of Ambrosius Marlianus, *Theatrum Politicum* into Greek. Another work, Περὶ καθηκόντων was printed in Bucharest in 1719 and in Leipzig in 1722. Nikolaos Mavrokordatos, with the help of the Patriarch of Jerusalem Chrysanthos Notaras, reorganized the Authentike Akademia in Jassy where many Greek scholars of note taught. It was in the service of the Phanariots, first in Constantinople and later in Rumania that Regas Velestinles came into contact with French culture and French revolutionary ideas.

The Greek Enlightenment is subdivided into three periods. The first (1750–1774) was dominated by the introduction and influence of Voltaire into Greece through the translations of Eugenios Voulgaris and others. Iosepos Moisiodax (1725–1800) was the most important figure of this period. The second period (1774–1820), the mature phase of the Greek movement, was greatly influenced by the French Encyclopedists. There were a large number of translations into Greek of scientific, philosophical and mathematical works and a great interest in education. During this time Demetrios Katartzes (c. 1730–1807) and his followers—among them Regas Velestinles—were active, and it was also during this time that the Γεωγραφία νεωτερική of Daniel Philippides and Gregorios Konstantas was published. The third and final phase is dominated by the figure of Adamantios Koraes and his circle.

31. Theophilos Korydalleus, c. 1563–1646. Περὶ ἐπιστολικῶν τύπων [Ἔκθεσις περὶ ῥητορικῆς]. London, G. Stansby 1625.

Theophilos Korydalleus was born in Athens. His family name was Skordelos but he changed it to Korydalleus, also spelled Korydaleus, in order to make it more archaic in sound. After completing his studies in Athens he went to Italy, where he studied at the Collegio Greco di San Atanasio in Rome and then at the University of Padua. In Padua he studied philosophy and medicine. In 1609 he accepted the

teaching post at the Greek school operated by the Greek community of Venice and remained in Venice teaching until 1614. He subsequently returned to Athens and in 1615 began teaching there. His subjects included astronomy and philosophy. He also held teaching posts in the Ionian Islands in Kephallenia and Zakynthos where he not only taught the above mentioned subjects but also practiced medicine. It was during his stay in Zakynthos that he entered the priesthood and was given the name Theodosios. However, shortly afterwards he renounced the cloth and threw away his habit.

In c.1625 the patriarch of Constantinople Kyrillos Loukaris wished to revitalize the curriculum of the Patriarchal Academy and invited Theophilos Korydalleus to direct it. Korydalleus stayed in Constantinople until 1640, at which time he was ordained Metropolitan of Naupaktos and Arta. He served at his new post for only one year and then for unknown reasons asked to be released from his duties. He later returned to Athens where he resumed the teaching of philosophy. Korydalleus was well known as a teacher and attracted many pupils from all over Greece. He died in 1646.

Korydalleus was the foremost philosopher of what is known in Greek letters as the period of Church Humanism (1600–1669). His influence extended beyond Greece to other Balkan nations, especially Rumania. The initiator and strongest supporter of the movement was the Patriarch Kyrillos Loukaris, who wished to improve the education of the Greek clergy and tried to bring to Constantinople men of letters to reform the curriculum of the Patriarchal Academy and make Constantinople the center of Orthodoxy and Hellenism.

The whole oeuvre of Theophilos Korydalleus was based on the commentary of Aristotle and the teaching of neo-Aristotelian philosophy. Korydalleus's commentaries on Aristotle circulated in manuscript form and to this day many of these survive in libraries all over Greece and Rumania. Korydalleus was important as an educator and offered a great service in the philosophical education of the Greeks. He was the first Greek thinker to combat scholasticism and to separate philosophy from theology. However, his followers carried what became known as Korydalism to great extremes and it later came to represent a term of deprecation and was attacked by the later exponents of the Greek Enlightenment.

The above work, his first to appear in print, was edited by one of his pupils, Nikodemos Metaxas, who was in England at the time learning the art of printing and buying printing types and equipment to take to Constantinople.

1962–C. T. Keller Fund.

32. Alexandros Mavrokordatos, 1641–1709. Ἱστορία ἱερά ἤτοι, Τὰ Ἰουδαϊκά. Ἐν Βουκουρεστίῳ, παρὰ Ἀνθίμου τοῦ ἐξ Ἰβηρίας 1716.

Alexandros Mavrodordatos was born in Constantinople, the son of Nikolaos and Roxane or Roxandra Skarlatou. The family was originally from Chios. His mother was well-educated, a pupil of Ioannes Karyophyllis and is considered by many scholars to have been the first Greek woman intellectual of the *Tourkokratia*.

At an early age Alexandros was sent to study at the Greek College of San Atanasio in Rome and later at the Universities of Padua and Bologna, where he earned degrees in philosophy and medicine. His doctoral dissertation on the circulation of the blood, *Pneumaticum instrumentum circulandi sanguinis*, was published in Bologna in 1664, in Frankfurt in 1665 and again in Leipzig in 1682. Upon the completion of his studies Alexandros returned to Constantinople and practiced medicine. He also taught with success at the Patriarchal Academy. In 1671 he became the secretary of Panayotakis Nikousios, who was the Grand Dragoman of the Turkish government. In 1673 Alexandros Mavrokordatos succeeded Nikousios as Secretary of State of the Turkish Empire, where his education and especially his knowledge of many languages—besides Greek, Latin, and Italian he also spoke Turkish, Arabic and Persian—was of great help in his new position.

After Alexandros Mavrokordatos negotiated the treaty of Karlowitz (1699), the Turkish government conferred on him the title Exaporite (Ἐξ Ἀπορρήτων). His influence with the Turkish government was considerable and he was able to ease the conditions of the Christian subjects of the Turkish Empire. For his many services to the Orthodox Church Mavrokordatos was given the title of *Megas Logothetes*.

Mavrokordatos left a voluminous correspondence

and other works, most of which remained in manuscript form. Besides his *Pseumaticum instrumentum*, which was published during his lifetime, all other works, such as the Ἱστορία ἱερά (1716), Γραμματικὴ περὶ συντάξεως (1745), and Φροντίσματα (1805), were published posthumously. The *Historia hiera*, a history of the Jews, was edited and published at the expense of his son Ioannes Nikolaos Mavrokordatos (1670–1730) who was at the time Voivode of Wallachia. It was the last work to appear from the press of Antim of Ivir.

1971–L. M. Friedman Fund.

33. Eugenios Voulgaris, Abp. of Slovensk and Cherson, 1716–1806. Ἡ λογική. Ἐν Λειψίᾳ τῆς Σαξονίας, ἐν τῇ τυπογραφίᾳ τοῦ Βρεϊτκόπφ 1766.

Eugenios Voulgaris was born in Corfu from a family originally from Zakynthos and was christened Eleutherios. He received his primary and secondary education in Corfu where he studied under the supervision of Antonios Katephoros. Some maintain that he studied at the school in Arta before going to Ioannina in Epirus. It was while in Ioannina in 1737 or 1738 that he received orders, becoming a deacon and being given the name Eugenios. It is believed that he went to study in Padua, where traditionally most Greeks received their higher education. At Padua he studied philosophy and came into contact with the philosophical ideas of Locke, Leibniz and Wolff. Voulgaris was also interested in the sciences, especially physics and mathematics. He returned to Ioannina in 1742 and became the head of the newly established Maroutsaia Academy. His teaching, which included the introduction of modern philosophy into his lectures, was attacked by the conservative teachers of the school, who accused him of introducing dangerous ideas into the curriculum. In 1750 Voulgaris resigned his post and accepted the directorship of the school in Kozani. His reputation as a teacher reached Constantinople and in 1753 the Patriarch Kyrillos VI appointed him head of the newly established (1750) school of Mount Athos, the Athonias Academy. Among his pupils there were Athanasios Parios, Iosepos Moisiodax and Sergios Makraios, who later became teachers of note in their own right. The years of his tenure at the Athonias Academy were very productive for Voulgaris. Besides teaching he translated John Locke's *Essay*, Christian Wolff's *Elements of Geometry* and many other works which circulated among his pupils in manuscript form.

After a residence of almost six years at the Athonias Academy Voulgaris was invited by the Patriarch Serapheim II to join the teaching staff of the Patriarchal Academy in Constantinople, where he taught for three years. Again his teaching came under attack and when Patriarch Serapheim II was no longer on the patriarchal throne Voulgaris left his post. In 1763 he went to Germany via the Danubian principalities and spent eight years there, mostly in Leipzig. It was in Leipzig that he finally published some of his works and his translations. In 1766 he brought out his most important work, Ἡ λογική which consisted of his lectures in philosophy. Until then his work had circulated only in manuscript form. Voulgaris was the first to introduce the works of Voltaire to the Greeks with his translation of *Essai historique sur les dissensions des églises de Pologne* (Περὶ τῶν διχονοιῶν τῶ ἐνταῖς ἐκκλησίαις τῆς Πολονίας) which appeared in 1768. Voulgaris' reputation as a scholar and representative of the new philosophy had reached the court circles in Russia and in 1772 Catherine the Great invited him to join her court. For three years he was her librarian and adviser. He was later ordained an hieromonachos and then in 1776 as Archbishop of Slovensk and Cherson in the Ukraine, but in 1779 he resigned this post in favor of another Corfiote teacher and monk, Nikephoros Theotokes. Voulgaris himself returned to St. Petersburg and remained there until 1802, at which time he retired to the monastery of Saint Alexander Nevsky where he died in 1806.

Although Eugenios Voulgaris did not again teach in Greece after his departure from Constantinople, his publications played an important role in the education of Greeks everywhere. Voulgaris has been considered the precursor of the Greek Enlightenment, the bridge between the old and the new eras, and he is regarded as one of the most important teachers of the nation (Διδάσκαλος τοῦ Γένους).

1974–Duplicate Fund.

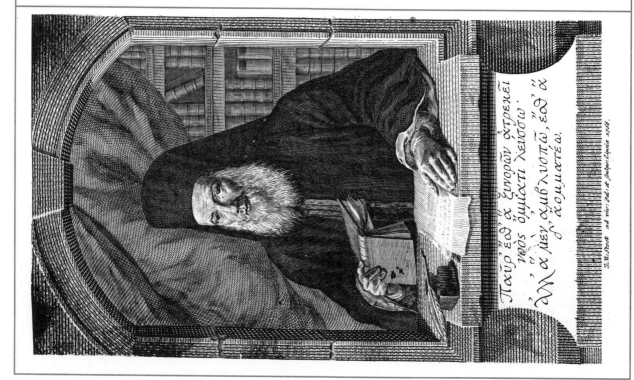

33

ΛΕΞΙΚΟΝ ΤΡΙΓΛΩΣΣΟΝ

τῆς

Γαλλικῆς, Ἰταλικῆς, καὶ Ρωμαικῆς διαλέκτου εἰς τρεῖς τόμους διῃρημένον.

Ἐκπονηθὲν

ΓΕΩΡΓΙΟΥ ΒΕΝΤΟΤΗ.

Ἐπιταγῇ μὲν καὶ φιλοτίμῳ δαπάνῃ, τοῦ ΥΨΗΛΟΤΑΤΟΥ, ΚΑΙ ΓΑΛΗΝΟΤΑΤΟΥ ΠΡΙΓΚΙΠΟΣ ΜΟΛΔΟΒΛΑΧΙΑΣ.

ΚΥΡΙΟΥ ΚΥΡΙΟΥ

ΑΛΕΞΑΝΔΡΟΥ ΙΩΑΝΝΟΥ τοῦ ΜΑΥΡΟΚΟΡΔΑΤΟΥ

Συνδρομῇ δὲ καὶ φιλοπόνῳ σπουδῇ, τοῦ Ἠμωτάτε ἐν Πραγματευταῖς

ΚΥΡΙΟΥ

ΔΗΜΗΤΡΙΟΥ ΠΑΥΛΟΥ

Εὐπατρίδε, ἐν τῇ Ἡ. ἐν τῆς πόλεως διαπεπραγματευσαμένου Ἰωαννίνων.

ΤΟΜΟΣ Α΄.

ΓΑΛΛΟ-ΡΩΜΑΙΚΟ-ΙΤΑΛΙΚΟΣ.

FRANÇOIS, GREC, & ITALIEN.

Ἐν Βιέννῃ τῆς Αουστρίας 1790.

Ἐκ τῆς Τυπογραφίας Ἰωσήφου τοῦ ΒΑΟΥΜΕΙΣΤΕΡΟΥ.

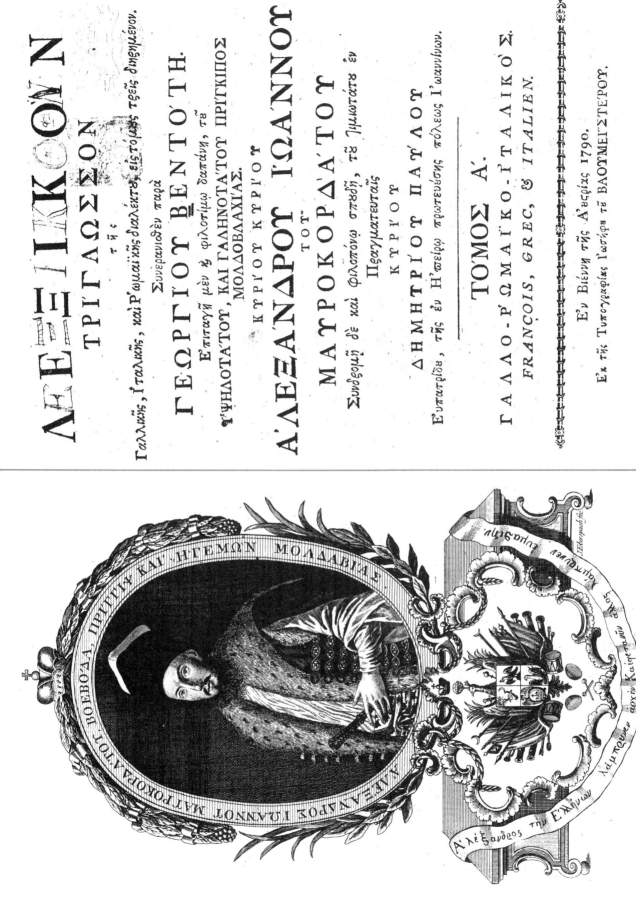

ΒΟΕΒΟΔΑ, ΠΡΙΓΚΙΨ ΚΑΙ ΗΓΕΜΩΝ ΜΟΛΔΑΒΙΑΣ.

ΑΛΕΞΑΝΔΡΟΣ ΙΩΑΝΝΟΥ ΜΑΥΡΟΚΟΡΔΑΤΟΥ

Ἀλέξανδρος τῇ Ἑλλάδι λάμπεσθαι ἀρχιερατείαν Καίσαρέων χοῦ

34. Georgios Ventotes, 1757–1795. *Λεξικὸν τρίγλωσσον.* Ἐν Βιέννῃ τῆς Ἀουστρίας, ἐκ τῆς τυπογραφίας Ἰωσήφου τοῦ Βαουμεϊστέρου 1790.

This trilingual dictionary of French, Greek, and Italian was compiled by Georgios Ventotes and printed at the expense and command of Alexandros Ioannou Mavrokordatos (1754–1819), Voivode of Moldavia, whose portrait appears in the first volume. Georgios Ventotes went to Vienna from his native Zakynthos after a sojourn in Venice, where from 1777 to 1780 he served as translator and corrector at the press of Nikolaos Glykys. Ventotes finally settled in Vienna, where his many-faceted talents as translator, editor and finally founder and director of his own press were realized. At the beginning of his Vienna career Ventotes worked for the noted Austrian publisher Joseph Baumeister, for whom he translated into modern Greek several works from the French and German which were printed at the press of Baumeister with the financial backing of Polyzois Lampanitziotis. It was during this period that Ventotes also published a grammar of the French language (1786) and his translation of William Robertson's *The History of America* (1792–1794). He also edited many other Greek works which were published by Baumeister.

Ventotes was a pioneer in another field. He was the first to publish a Greek semi-weekly newspaper. It came out in 1784 and its publication, lasting approximately two months, was suspended at the request of the Turkish government, which protested to the Austrian Ambassador in Constantinople that the newspaper was creating great unrest among its subjects. Although no trace of this newspaper has been found to date there are ample documents in the Austrian archives and in other sources which speak of its existence. Another of Ventotes' firsts was the publication of Greek calendars beginning with the year 1789. In 1791 he succeeded in obtaining permission to open his own printing establishment and was very active in publishing Greek books until his untimely death in 1795. The Ventotes press continued to operate under his name until 1810 when the press was sold by his widow to Johann Bartholomaeus Zweck or Zweek, who had been in charge of the press for some time.

1908 – The gift of Mary Bryant Brandegee in memory of William Fletcher Weld.

35. Daniel Philippides & Gregorios Konstantas, *Γεωγραφία νεωτερική.* Ἐν Βιέννῃ, Παρὰ Θωμᾷ τῷ Τράττνερν 1791.

Daniel Philippides (1775–1832) and Gregorios Konstantas (1758–1844) were both from Melies, a village on Mount Pelion in Thessaly, and along with Anthimos Gazes (1764–1828) comprise what is known as the School of Melies. Both Philippides and Konstantas had travelled extensively and spent some time in the Danubian Principalities. After his studies at the Athonias School Philippides taught at Jassy at the *Authentike Schole* before spending some years in Vienna. He also went to Paris where he met Lalande and Barbier du Bocage. He made a number of translations from the French into modern Greek, among them the *Logic* of Condillac and the book on astronomy by Lalande. He also wrote a history and geography of Rumania. Like Philippides, Konstantas was also educated at the Athonias school and later spent some time in Chios, Constantinople and Bucharest. He also taught at the *Authentike Schole* in Jassy. He then spent four years in Vienna and also studied at Padua. He had a long and distinguished career as a teacher and founded along with Anthimos Gazes a school at Melies.

Konstantas was also active in education during the Greek War of Independence and during the governorship of Ioannes Kapodistrias (1827–1831). He was the main person responsible for the introduction of the Lancasterian method or Mutual Instruction method of teaching into Greece.

The geography of Philippides and Konstantas broke new ground by introducing the physical characteristics of Greece's natural history and by providing information about the political and economic conditions of contemporary societies, their judicial systems and their social structures. It examined their religions, educational systems, and languages and compared them with the existing conditions in Greece. This was a novel way of teaching geography. Only the first volume of a projected three was published. The other two, which remained in manuscript form, were destroyed in a fire in 1795. The authors made a strong appeal for the use and recognition of the modern language in education, but the publication of their *Γεωγραφία νεωτερική* was not received favorably by the educators and academics of their time and it was

ΓΕΩΓΡΑΦΙΑ
ΝΕΩΤΕΡΙΚΗ.

ΒΙΒΛΙΟΝ
ΠΡΩΤΟΝ
Περὶ Τῆς Γηΐνης Σφαίρας ἐν Γένει. (α)

Ἡ Γῆ ὁπȣ κατοικȣμεν δὲν εἶναι μιὰ πεδιάδα
ἐξαπλωμένη ἐπ᾽ ἄπειρο καθὼς μᾶς φαίνεται, ἀμὴ εἶναι σχεδὸν σφαῖρα (διὰ τȣτο
κỳ σφαιροειδῆ τὴ λέγομεν) περικυκλωμένη ἀπὸ
ὅλα της τὰ μέρη ἀπὸ ἀέρα.
                                                   Διὰ

(α) Ἑκαταῖος ὁ Μιλήσιος ἐξέδωκε πρῶτος γεωγραφικὸ σύγ-
γρμμμα. Στράβων βιϐ. ά.
     Σφαῖρα λέγεται ἕνα σῶμα ὁλοςρόγγυλο , καθὼς εἶναι τỳ
τόπι, ὁπȣ παίζȣν τὰ παιδιά. Σῶμα εἶναι κάθοτὶ ὁπȣ ὑποκίηται
                                       Λ

35

rejected for school use, even though it was the only book at the time that offered a comprehensive geographical study of Greece. It was left for later generations to appreciate the innovative intellectual achievement of the *Modern Geography* and to recognize its place in the Greek Enlightenment movement.

1964 – C. T. Keller Fund.

36. Athanasios Psalidas, 1767–1829. Ἀληθὴς εὐδαιμονία ἤτοι βάσις πάσης θρησκείας. *Vera felicitas sive fundamentum omnis religionis.* Viennae, In typographia Baumeisteriana 1791.

This work of Athanasios Psalidas was written when its author was only twenty-four. It was written in Modern Greek "εἰς τὴν ἁπλῆν διάλεκτον" and was translated into Latin by the author.

Athanasios Psalidas was born in Ioannina of well-to-do parents. In 1785 he went to Russia to join his older brothers and to study first at Nizna and later in Poltava in the Ukraine. In 1787 he went to Vienna to further his education and was enrolled in the School of Medicine at the university, but abandoned his medical studies to pursue studies in philosophy and the physical sciences. He remained in Vienna until 1795 and then returned to Ioannina where he began his long career as a teacher. He taught at the Maroutsaian Academy and when the school closed down because of lack of funds he was able to raise funds to begin a school of his own, the Kaplanaia School, which during the years of Psalidas' tenure as director (1796–1820) became famous for the quality of teaching and the subjects taught there. During this period Epirus was ruled by Ali Pasha of Tepelen, who thought highly of Psalidas and sought his advice in matters of diplomacy and relied upon Psalidas' knowledge of foreign languages. Because of the good relationship he enjoyed with Ali Pasha, Psalidas was spared when he was formally accused for his teaching methods and forward looking ideas by the conservative teachers of the Balanos School in Ioannina who maintained that Psalidas was an atheist and a disciple of Voltaire.

In August 1820 when Turkey launched an attack on Ali Pasha, Psalidas left Ioannina and in 1822 moved to Corfu. When in 1823 the Ionian Academy was founded in Corfu by Lord Guilford, Psalidas was not offered a professorship, although some of his own pupils were. Finally, in 1828 he became the principal of a Lyceum on the island of Leukas and died there the following year.

Psalidas left behind a voluminous oeuvre, most of which remained and circulated in manuscript form. Many of the travellers to Greece of this period who visited the court of Ali Pasha made the acquaintance of Psalidas and commented about him in their travelogues. Edward Everett visited Ioannina in 1819 and met Psalidas. He speaks of Psalidas and his school and was impressed by the fact that the school was financed by wealthy Greeks and not by the government. He also mentions that Psalidas offered him a copy of his book, "The True Happiness". Another American who visited Ioannina and met Psalidas was Theodore Lyman, who wrote about his visit in the *North American Review* in 1820.

1965 – Patrick Grant II Fund (HC 1908)

37. Regas Velestinles, c. 1757–1798, ed. & tr. Ὁ ἠθικὸς τρίπους. Ἐν Ὀφένῃ, Ἐν τῷ τυπογραφείῳ τοῦ Πανδιδακτηρίου 1815.

Regas was the Protomartyr of the Greek Revolution. No other figure gripped the imagination of the Greek people as he did. He was born in Velestino in Thessaly and went to school either in nearby Zagora on Mount Pelion or in Ampelakia. He later went to Constantinople to seek employment and further his education. While in Constantinople he worked as secretary to Alexandros Hypselantes and through Phanariot connections he came into contact with French culture and French revolutionary ideas. He also learned the French, German and Italian languages.

In 1786 Regas went to Bucharest in Wallachia and became the secretary of the ruling prince Nikolaos Mavrogenes. In 1790 Regas became the secretary of Baron de Langefeld and followed him to Vienna, the most active center of the Greek Diaspora during this period. It had supplanted Venice in printing the important books. It was also in Vienna that wealthy Greek merchants were active in financing resistance groups to the Turks. There were societies founded to discuss ways and means to liberate the Greeks from Turkish rule. It was during this first visit that some of Regas' works and translations were published. His first work to appear was a collection of six short stories translated from the French entitled Σχολεῖον τῶν ντελικάτων ἐραστῶν. Another work published during this period was his φυσικῆς ἀπάνθισμα. Both works were translated into modern Greek. Regas returned to Wallachia in 1791 and remained there until 1796. It was during this period that he made the acquaintance of Émile Gaudin, a young French diplomat who was very active in gaining friends and disciples to the revolutionary new ideas emanating from France. Regas, who had always been an admirer of the French

ΤΜΗΜΑ ΠΡΩΤΟΝ.

ΠΕΡΙ

ΥΠΑΡΞΕΩΣ ΘΕΟΥ.

§. 36.

,, Πρὸ τȣ̃ λοιπὸν νὰ εἰσχωρέσωμεν εἰς αὐτὴν τὴν ἰδέαν τȣ̃ Θεȣ, ὁπȣ̃ τῶρα ἔχομεν, πρέπει νὰ κάμωμεν κᾄποιαν θεωρίαν ἐπ' ὀλίγον διὰ νὰ στοχασθῶμεν οίας λογῆς εἶναι αἱ ἰδέαι, ὡσαύτως καὶ ἐπάνω εἰς τὴν ἰδίαν τȣ̃ Θεȣ̃, ἡ ὁποία θεωρία θέλει ὑπηρετήσει καὶ εἰς τὰ ἄ҃α τρία Τμήματα τȣ̃ παρόντος Βιβλιαρίȣ. ''

§. 37.

,, Ὁ ἄνθρωπος λοιπὸν, ὁπȣ̃ εἶναι τὸ πλέον τιμιώτερον ἀπὸ ὅλα τὰ ἐν τῇ γῇ ζῶα, ὁ ὁποῖος ὀνομάζεται λογικὸς, καθ' ὅ τῶν ἄλλων ζώων διαφέρει, αὐτὸς εἶναι συνδȣτὸς ἐκ δυοῖν ȣσιῶν, ἐκ πνευματικῆς δηλαδὴ καὶ ὑλικῆς ἤτοι ἐκ ψυχῆς καὶ σώματος. Αὗται αἱ δύο ȣσίαι εἶναι πολλᾷ διαφορετικαὶ δυνάμεις. Καὶ ἡ μὲν ψυχὴ πε-ρι᷎-

Enlightenment, became close friends with Gaudin.

By 1796 Regas was back in Vienna, where he printed his map of Greece (*Χάρτα τῆς Ἑλλάδος*) in 1797 and his translations of Metastasio, Marmontel, the abbé Barthélemy and others. He also printed his patriotic and revolutionary pamphlets urging the Greeks to take up arms against the Turks. His *Θούριος*, which is a revolutionary call to arms in verse, has been incorporated into the collections of the folk-poetry of Greece; and children to this day memorize it at school. The Austrian authorities arrested Regas and seven of his followers in Trieste, accusing them of belonging to a secret society. They turned them over to the Turkish authorities in Belgrade, who on 24 June 1798 executed them and threw their bodies into the Danube.

The translations contained in this volume were first printed in Vienna in 1797. They include Regas' translations of Pietro Metastasio's *Olimpiade*, and J. F. Marmontel's *Bergère des Alpes*. Salomon Gessner's *Der erste Schiffer*, was translated by Antonios Koronios, one of Regas' followers who was also executed in 1798.

1887 – Bequest of Professor E. A. Sophocles.

38. Ἑρμῆς ὁ λόγιος.   Ἐν Βιέννῃ τῆς Ἀουστρίας, Ἐκ τῆς τυπογραφίας τοῦ Ἰω. Βαρθολ. Τζβεκίου, πρώην Βενδώτου 1811 – 1821.

This first journal in modern Greek was published in Vienna under the editorship of Anthimos Gazes (1764–1828) who was the priest of the Greek church of St. George in Vienna and an editor and translator of note. The journal was partly subsidized by the newly-founded Philological Society of the Greek Lyceum of Bucharest. The appearance of *Ἑρμῆς ὁ λόγιος* was favorably received and was reviewed in foreign journals such as the *Annalen der Literatur und Kunst* (Vienna, June 1811). In 1816 the editorial duties of the journal were taken over by Theokletos Pharmakides (1784–1860), and Konstantinos Kokkinakes (1781–1831), both ardent followers of Adamantios Koraes. From the outset, the periodical sought to inform its readership about the ideas of Greeks everywhere who were trying to guide and instruct the nation and also to impart the new trends in literature, science and education of Enlightened Europe, especially France, to their co-nationals. Its correspondents and contributors were the intellectuals who lived in the various centers of the Greek Diaspora. The journal also reported on the writings about Greece and the Greeks found in the various books of foreign travellers to the Eastern Mediterranean, such as those of Leake, Holland, Choiseul-Gouffier, and others.

The journal was widely distributed and reached as far as Boston and Philadelphia. It ceased publication shortly after the outbreak of the Greek War of Independence. *Ἑρμῆς ὁ λόγιος* became the model for other pre-revolutionary journals such as *Μέλισσα* (Paris, 1819–1821), *Καλλιόπη* (Vienna, 1819–1821), and *Ἀθηνᾶ* (Paris, 1819).

Early acquisition — Source unknown.

38

Greek War of Independence

The Greek uprising against Ottoman rule was prepared by the activities of the Philike Hetaireia (Friendly Society) which was founded in Odessa in 1814. In 1820 Alexandros Hypselantes, who at the time was the aide to Ioannis Kapodistrias (1776–1831), Secretary of State to the Tsar, agreed to become the head of the Philike Hetaireia. Members of the clergy, wealthy landowners, and local chieftains joined the Hetaireia in ever increasing numbers to prepare for the Greek Revolution. Hypselantes' plan was to train a select force in the Danubian principalities to rise against the Turks, hopefully with the assistance of Russia. However, before the miliatary preparations were completed the members of the Hetaireia in the Morea (Peloponnese) asked Hypselantes to attack immediately while the Turks were engaged in fighting the forces of Ali Pasha in Albania. Hypselantes and his forces attacked on March 6, 1821 but were defeated handily. It was not until about March 25 — considered the traditional date for the beginning of the Greek War of Independence — that sporadic attacks began in the Morea. Immediate reprisals by the Turks resulted in the massacre of Greeks in Asia Minor and on April 22 the hanging of the Patriarch of Constantinople Gregorios V.

The naval battle of Navarino on October 20, 1827, where the forces of Great Britain, France, and Russia defeated the Turkish fleet, made the liberation of Greece a virtual certainty. However, two more years passed before the fighting ended on the Greek mainland. Ioannis Kapodistrias, who was elected provisional president of Greece by the third National Assembly in April 1827, arrived to take up office soon after.

39. Adamantios Koraes, 1748–1833. *Σάλπισμα πολεμιστήριον. 2. ἔκδ. διορθωμένη μὲ προσθήκη εἰς τὸ τέλος. Ἐν Πελοποννήσῳ Ἐκ τῆς Ἑλληνικῆς τυπογραφίας Ἀτρομήτου τοῦ Μαραθωνίου* [Paris] 1821.

40. ———. *Τί συμφέρει εἰς τὴν ἐλευθερομένην ἀπὸ Τούρκους Ἑλλάδα νὰ πράξῃ εἰς τὰς παρούσας περιστάσεις διὰ νὰ μὴν δουλωθῇ εἰς χριστιανοὺς τουρκίζοντας. Διάλογος δύο Γραικῶν. Ἐν Ναυπλίῳ* [Paris] 1830.

Adamantios Koraes was the foremost proponent of the Greek Enlightenment. He was born in Smyrna of parents that came from the island of Chios. After completing his education in Smyrna he spent some years in Amsterdam (1771–1778) in the silk trade, but he returned to Smyrna because he found himself unsuited to a career in business. In 1782 he went to Montpellier, where he studied medicine. After completing his studies he moved to Paris in 1788, arriving the year before the outbreak of the French Revolution. He never returned to Greece because, as he said, life under Turkish domination was unacceptable for him.

Koraes' approach to the regeneration of the Greek nation was through the study of Greek culture — ancient philosophy, history and literature — while assimilating at the same time the new trends in European science and philosophy. In 1805 he embarked on a systematic publication of ancient Greek texts with long introductions expounding his ideas and theories on education and language. His entire oeuvre, some twenty volumes or more, was dedicated to his country's need for self-realization. Besides his editions of the classics, he left behind a voluminous correspondence, addresses, and memoranda, as well as political and nationalistic writings.

Koraes was very interested in education and was always urging the establishment of more schools and libraries in Greece. He was also very concerned with the problem of language in education. He believed in taking the middle road and advocated the use of a simple *katharevousa*. This was opposed by the

Ὤμοι ἐγὼ πανάπωτμος, ἐπεί μ' ἕλε δούλιον ἤμαρ.

ΣΑΛΠΙΣΜΑ
ΠΟΛΕΜΙΣΤΗΡΙΟΝ.

ΔΕΥΤΕΡΑ ΕΚΔΟΣΙΣ,

ΔΙΩΡΘΩΜΕΝΗ, ΚΑΙ ΗΥΞΗΜΕΝΗ ΜΕ ΠΡΟΣΘΗΚΗΝ ΕΙΣ ΤΟ ΤΕΛΟΣ.

...... Μείζον' ἔτις ἀντὶ τῆς αὐτοῦ ΠΑΤΡΑΣ
φίλον κομίζει, τοῦτον οὐδαμοῦ λέγω.
ΣΟΦΟΚΛ. Ἀντιγ. στ. 182.

Ε'Ν ΠΕΛΟΠΟΝΝΗ'ΣΩΙ,
Ε'κ τῆς ἑλληνικῆς τυπογραφίας Ἀτρομήτου τοῦ
Μαραθωνίου.
1821.

39

demoticists, followers of the spoken Greek who insisted that the only way the masses were to be educated was for the intellectuals to write in the spoken language understood by all. At the other extreme from the demoticists were the arch-traditionalists, who adhered to a language that remained as close to ancient Greek as possible and was purged of all foreign influences.

Although Koraes' editions of the Greek classics are well known, his political pamphlets are much less so and far more rare. For the most part, they were published anonymously like the two on display here.

The Σάλπισμα πολεμιστήριον was first printed in 1801 when Napoleon and the French army were in Egypt and stirred up ideas of freedom among the Greeks. It came out in this second, enlarged edition in 1821. In it, Koraes asserts that freedom for the Greeks must be followed by equality in order to be just. The work was printed in Paris (not in the Peloponnese as stated on the titlepage).

The second work, known as the Διάλογος δύο Γραικῶν, was also published anonymously in Paris (not in Nauplia). It came out after Greece had gained its independence, during the turbulent years of the Kapodistrias era. In it Koraes expresses his fear that the Greek nation was veering away from the democratic form of government he valued. The work was written in the form of a dialogue between two Greeks.

1856–The bequest of Henry Ware Wales, M.D. of Boston (HC 1838).

41. Προσωρινὸν Πολίτευμα τῆς Ἑλλάδος. 1. ἔκδ. Ἐν Κορίνθῳ 1822.

As soon as the Greek War of Independence broke out in 1821 its leaders, especially Demetrios Hypselantes, were aware that they would need not only arms but also a means to issue proclamations. A small press was brought from Trieste to Greece in June 1821. However, until a printer could be found to operate it the press remained idle and the first proclamations of the revolution circulated in manuscript form. After the destruction of the Kydonies press, Konstantinos Tompras, the printer who had trained at the Didot firm in Paris, escaped to the island of Psara and from there joined Hypselantes and the press that was at the time in Astros. The press finally began operating in Kalamata. This was the only press available during 1821. Besides various proclamations it also printed the first newspaper on Greek soil, the Σάλπιγξ Ἑλληνική. The press followed Hypselantes and his

men from place to place in the Peloponnese.

Meanwhile, a second press arrived in Corinth from Livorno. This press too was under the direction of Konstantinos Tompras and his aide Anastasios Nikolaïdes. It was with this second press that the first edition of the Provisional Constitution of Greece was printed in 1822. Both presses were destroyed or left behind in July 1822 when the city was attacked and taken over by the Turkish forces under Dramali.

The representatives of all sections of the country came to Epidaurus on January 1, 1822 for the first National Convention and under the leadership of Alexandros Mavrokordatos and with Theodoros Negris as General Secretary wrote and ratified the Προσωρινὸν Πολίτευμα τῆς Ἑλλάδος.

1858 – Purchased November 1858 for the sum of 1 drachma.

42. Franceso Bruno, Physician to Lord Byron. *Cenni sui mezzi più atti a mantennere sani i soldati in campagna.* Περὶ τῶν μέσων . . . εἰς τὴν διατήρησιν τῆς ὑγιείας τῶν στρατιωτῶν. Ἐν Μεσολογγίῳ, Ἐκ τῆς τυπογραφίας Δημητρίου Μεσθενέως 1824.

This is one of the first books brought out by the newly-established press at Missolonghi. This first press had been brought from France to Missolonghi by Alexandros Mavrokordatos and under Pavlos Patrikios it began operations by announcing on 18 December 1823 the forthcoming publication of the newspaper Ἑλληνικὰ Χρονικά, the first issue of which appeared on January 2, 1824.

Meanwhile a well-trained printer who had studied in France had arrived in Missolonghi. This was

Demetrios Mestheneus who took over the printing operations of the press. The pamphlet compiled by Francesco Bruno, a physician who accompanied Lord Byron to Greece, was the first product of the press after the Ἑλληνικὰ Χρονικά. It was also this press which printed the announcement of the death of Lord Byron and the Funeral Oration delivered on April 10 (Old Calendar) by Spyridon Trikoupis.

Received June 23, 1831 – Source unknown.

43. Προσωρινή Διοίκησις τῆς Ἑλλάδος. Ἐν Μεσολογγίῳ, 1824.

This broadside announces to the Greek people the death of Lord Byron of complications from rheumatic fever that had lasted ten days. It is dated Missolonghi, 7 April (Old Calendar) 1824 and signed by Alexandros Mavrokordatos. It sets forth the official preparations for mourning:

At daybreak on 8 April there will be a thirty-seven gun salute from the walls of the city, one for each of the years of Lord Byron's life.
All government offices will be closed for three days.

All shops will be closed except those selling food and medications. Music and dancing will be prohibited as well as any other kind of revelry during the period of mourning.
There will be a period of official mourning for twenty-one days.
There will be funeral orations in all churches.

George Gordon, Sixth Lord Byron (1788 – 1824) first visited Greece during 1809 when, like many other scions of wealthy families, he made the grand tour of Europe. During this trip he visited first Ioannina and

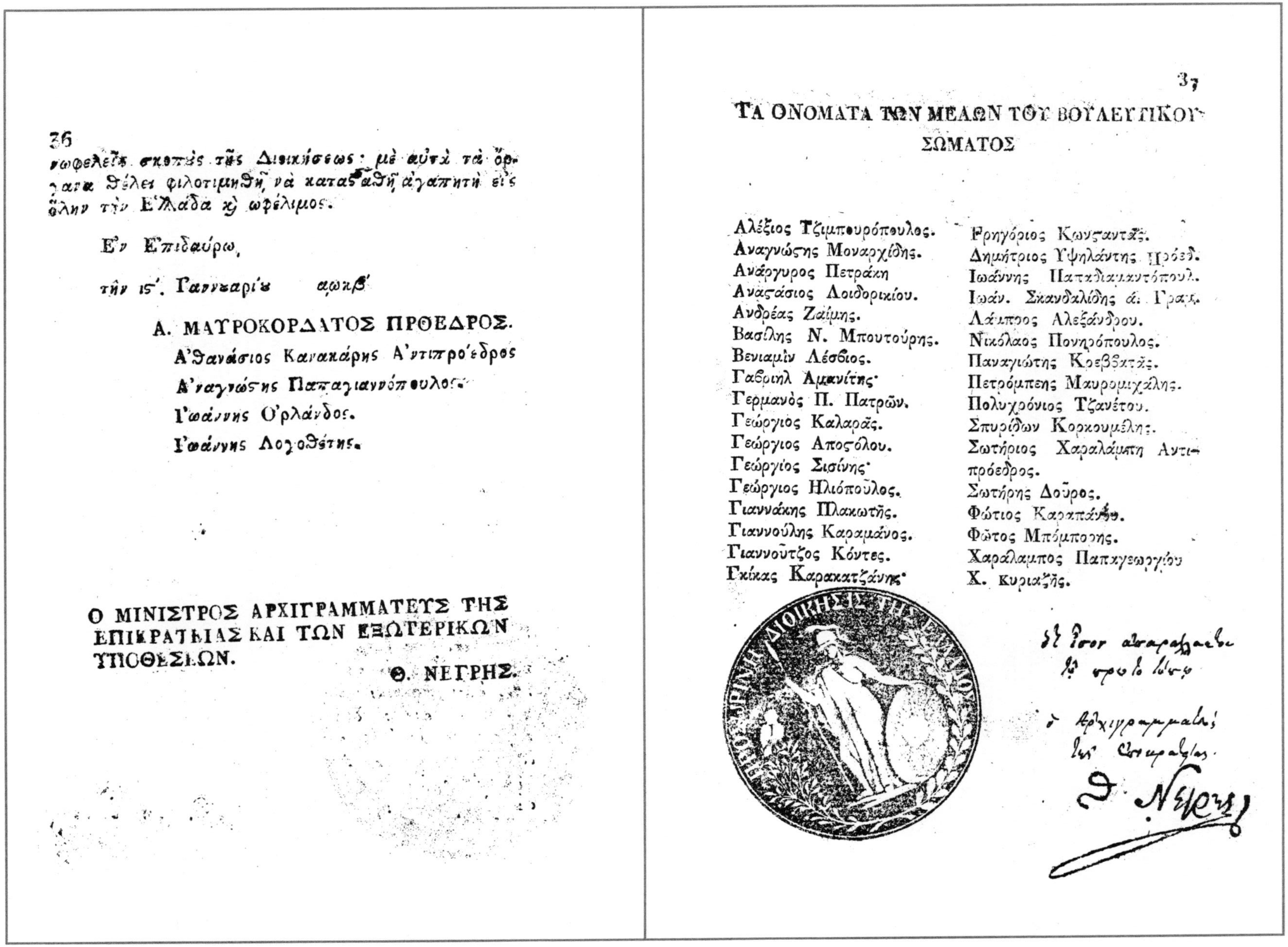

37

ΤΑ ΟΝΟΜΑΤΑ ΤΩΝ ΜΕΛΩΝ ΤΟΥ ΒΟΥΛΕΥΤΙΚΟΥ ΣΩΜΑΤΟΣ

Αλέξιος Τζιμπουρόπουλος.
Αναγνώστης Μοναρχίδης.
Ανάργυρος Πετράκη
Αναστάσιος Λοιδορικίου.
Ανδρέας Ζαΐμης.
Βασίλης Ν. Μπουτούρης.
Βενιαμίν Λέσβιος.
Γαβριήλ Αμανίτης·
Γερμανός Π. Πατρών.
Γεώργιος Καλαράς.
Γεώργιος Αποστόλου.
Γεώργιος Σισίνης·
Γεώργιος Ηλιόπουλος.
Γιαννάκης Πλακωτής·
Γιαννούλης Καραμάνος.
Γιαννούτζος Κόντες·
Γκίκας Καρακατζάνης·

Ρηγόπουλος Κωνσταντ.
Δημήτριος Υψηλάντης Πρόεδ.
Ιωάννης Παπαλεξαντόπουλ.
Ιωάν. Σκανδαλίδης ά. Γραμ.
Αχιλλεύς Αλεξάνδρου.
Νικόλαος Πουπρόπουλος.
Παναγιώτης Κρεββατάς·
Πετρόμπεης Μαυρομιχάλης.
Πολυχρόνιος Τζανέτου.
Σπυρίδων Κορκουμέλης·
Σωτήριος Χαραλάμπη Αντι-
πρόεδρος.
Σωτήρης Δούρος·
Φώτιος Καραπάνου.
Φώτος Μπόμποτης.
Χαράλαμπος Παπαγεωργίου
Χ. Κυριαζής.

41

νοφελεῖς σκοπὸς τῆς Διοικήσεως· μὲ αὐτὰ τὰ ὅρ-
ζατε θέλει φιλοτιμηθῆ νὰ καταστήσῃ ἀγαπητὴ εἰς
ὅλην τὴν Ἑλλάδα κὶ ὠφέλιμος.

Ἐν Ἐπιδαύρῳ,

τὴν ιϛ'. Γαμβηλιῶνος αωκβ'

Α. ΜΑΥΡΟΚΟΡΔΑΤΟΣ ΠΡΟΕΔΡΟΣ.

Ἀθανάσιος Κανακάρις Ἀντιπρόεδρος·
Ἀναγνώστης Παπαγιαννόπουλος·
Ἰωάννης Ὀρλάνδος.
Ἰωάννης Λογοθέτης·

Ο ΜΙΝΙΣΤΡΟΣ ΑΡΧΙΓΡΑΜΜΑΤΕΥΣ ΤΗΣ ΕΠΙΚΡΑΤΕΙΑΣ ΚΑΙ ΤΩΝ ΕΞΩΤΕΡΙΚΩΝ ΥΠΟΘΕΣΕΩΝ.

Θ. ΝΕΓΡΗΣ.

Ἀρ. 1185) ΠΡΟΣΩΡΙΝΗ ΔΙΟΙΚΗΣΙΣ ΤΗΣ ΕΛΛΑΔΟΣ.

Αἱ παροῦσαι χαρμόσυνοι ἡμέραι ἔγιναν διὰ ὅλους ἡμᾶς ἡμέραι πένθους.

Ὁ Λόρδ Νόελ Βυρὼν ἀπέρασε σήμερον εἰς τὴν ἄλλην ζωὴν περὶ τὰς ἕνδεκα ὥρας τὸ ἑσπέρας μετὰ μίαν ἀσθένειαν φλογιστικοῦ ῥευματικοῦ πυρετοῦ 10 ἡμερῶν.

Καὶ πρὶν ἀκόμη χωρισθῇ ἡ ψυχὴ ἀπὸ τὸ σῶμα, ἡ κοινὴ κατήφεια ἔλεγεν ὅσην θλίψιν ᾐσθάνετο ἡ καρδία ὅλων, καὶ ὅλοι μικροὶ μεγάλοι ἄνδρες καὶ γυναῖκες νικημένοι ἀπὸ τὴν θλίψιν, ἐλησμονήσατε τὸ Πάσχα.

Ἡ στέρησις αὐτοῦ τοῦ Λαμπροῦ ὑποκειμένου εἶναι βέβαια πολλὰ αἰσθαντικὴ δι' ὅλην τὴν Ἑλλάδα, ἀλλὰ εἶναι πολὺ περισσότερον ἀξιοθρήνητος διὰ αὐτὴν τὴν Πόλιν, τὴν ὁποίαν ἠγάπησε διαφερόντως, καὶ εἰς αὐτὴν ἐπολιτογράφη, καὶ ἀπόφασιν σταθερὰν εἶχεν ἂν τὸ ἔφερεν ἡ περίστασις νὰ γενῇ καὶ προσωπικῶς συμμέτοχος τῶν κινδύνων της.

Καθένας βλέπει ἐμπρός του τὰς πλουσίας πρὸς τὸ κοινὸν εὐεργεσίας του, καὶ μήτε ἔπαυσε μήτε παύει κάνεὶς μὲ εὐγνώμονα καὶ ἀληθινὴν φωνὴν νὰ τὸν ὀνομάζῃ εὐεργέτην.

Ἕως οὗ νὰ γνωστοποιηθοῦν αἱ διαταγαὶ τῆς Ἐθνικῆς Διοικήσεως περὶ αὐτοῦ τοῦ πολυθρηνήτου συμβάντος,

Δυνάμει τοῦ ὑπ' ἀρ. 314 καὶ ἡμ. 15 Ὀκτωβρίου θεσπίσματος τοῦ Βουλευτικοῦ Σώματος,

Διατάττεται,

ά.) Αὔριον μόλις ἀνατείλῃ ὁ Ἥλιος νὰ πέσουν ἀπὸ τὸ μεγάλον κανονοστάσιον τοῦ τείχους αὐτῆς τῆς Πόλεως 37 Κανονιαῖς (μία τὸ κάθε λεπτὸν) κατὰ τὸν ἀριθμὸν τῶν χρόνων τῆς ζωῆς τοῦ ἀποθανέντος.

β΄.) Ὅλα τὰ κοινὰ ὑπουργεῖα διὰ τρεῖς ἡμέρας κατὰ συνέχειαν νὰ κλεισθοῦν, ἐμπεριεχομένων καὶ τῶν κριτηρίων.

γ΄.) Νὰ κλεισθοῦν ὅλα τὰ ἐργαστήρια ἐκτὸς ἐκείνων, ὅπου πωλοῦνται τροφαί, καὶ ἰατρικά· καὶ νὰ λείψουν τὰ μουσικὰ παιγνήδια, οἱ συνειθισμένοι εἰς αὐτὰς τὰς ἡμέρας χοροί, νὰ παύσουν τὰ φαγοπότια εἰς τὰ κρασοπωλεῖα, καὶ κάθε ἄλλο εἶδος κοινοῦ ξεφαντώματος.

δ΄.) Νὰ γενῇ 21 ἡμέρας Γενικὴ πενθιφορία.

ε΄.) Νὰ γένουν ἐπικήδειοι δεήσεις εἰς ὅλας τὰς ἐκκλησίας.

Ἐν Μεσολογγίῳ τὴν 7 Ἀπριλλίου 1824.

Α. Μαυροκορδάτος.

Τ. Σ. Ὁ Γραμματεὺς
Γεώργιος Πραΐδης.

the court of Ali Pasha, then Missolonghi, Patras, and Athens, where he lodged with the family of Theodora Makri, whose daughter he immortalized as the *Maid of Athens*.

When the Greek Revolution broke out Byron made his second visit to Greece via the Ionian Islands and reached Missolonghi at the end of 1823, where he took under his command 500 Suliotes. He also distributed funds provided by the London Greek Committee. Alexandros Mavrokordatos, who was in charge of operations in Missolonghi, made him a colonel of artillery in the Greek army. However, his illness and sudden death cut short his attempts to serve Greece. His ardent support of the Greek cause helped enormously to persuade others to support Greece.

Alexandros Mavrokordatos (1791–1864) was a descendant of the well-known Phanariot family founded by his great great grandfather Alexandros Mavrokordatos the Exaporite (1641–1709). He took part in the Greek War of Independence and presided in January 1822 over the first Greek National Assembly as president of the executive in the Provisional Government of Greece. He served in successive Greek governments in various capacities including prime minister in 1841, 1844 and 1854–55.

1931–Friends of the Harvard College Library. Pencilled note: Recd this from the Προεοτό or Magistrate of Mycone, One of the Cyclades June the 1st 1824 J or I P.

44. Ἑλληνικά Χρονικά. Μεσολόγγιον, 6 Σεπτεμβρίου, 1824.

The Philhellenic Committee of London sent one of its members, Colonel Leicester Stanhope (1784–1862), to Greece to join Lord Byron and to also take to Greece four printing presses. Part of Colonel Stanhope's mission was to organize the postal service, but mainly it was to see that a free press was established. Colonel Stanhope arrived in Missolonghi in December 1823 while the presses were still en route. In Missolonghi he made the acquaintance of the Swiss Philhellene physician Johann Jacob Meyer and with his help Stanhope began plans to establish a newspaper there. While they were waiting for the printing equipment to arrive, Meyer with the help of Pavlos Patrikios began to bring out the newspaper Ἑλληνικά Χρονικά (Jan 1, 1824–Febr 20, 1826) using the small press which had been brought to

Missolonghi from France by Alexandros Mavrokordatos. Thus, the first thirty leaves (nos. 1–31) of the weekly newspaper were printed with the Mavrokordatos press. As soon as one of the presses from England arrived and was set up, Demetrios Mestheneus, a printer trained in France, began to print with the new, larger, and more up-to-date press.

Besides printing the Ἑλληνικά Χρονικά the press produced a series of small monographs. Both Johann Jacob Meyer and Demetrios Mestheneus lost their lives fighting during the Exodus of Missolonghi in 1826. The press was buried in the ruins of the town.

1856–The bequest of Henry Ware Wales M.D. of Boston (HC 1838)

45. Πολιτικὸν Σύνταγμα τῆς Ἑλλάδος. τυπογραφίας τῆς Κυβερνήσεως 1827. [Ἐν Ναυπλίῳ] Ἐκ τῆς

In March 1827 the Third National Assembly was convened in Troizen and its deliberations produced a new constitution, the Πολιτικὸν Σύνταγμα in which the reins of government were henceforth to be conferred on a governor, the Parliament and the Judiciary. It was based on the French model of government. The governor elected was Ioannis Kapodistrias (1776–1831) and his term of office was to be for seven years. It was also at this national assembly that it was decided to appoint Sir Richard Church (1784–1873) General in charge of the Greek armies and Thomas Cochrane (1775–1860)

Commander in Chief of the Greek navies. This document was printed by the newly-established Government Printing Office operating since 1825 out of Nauplia, which became the first capital of Modern Greece. It was also in Nauplia that the Γενικὴ Ἐφημερὶς τῆς Ἑλλάδος began publication on 7 October 1825.

The Government Printing Office moved at times from place to place whenever it was necessary. For example, during the deliberations of the National Assembly it was moved to nearby Poros and some issues of the Γενικὴ Ἐφημερὶς were printed there.

45

Later one part of the Government Printing Office operated in Aegina while the other was printing in Nauplia.

1878–The gift of Professor William Everett (HU 1859). The book bears the inscription in Greek "To Mr. E. Everett with the greetings of his friend S. G. Howe".

46. Theodoros Kolokotrones, 1770–1843. Ἑλληνικῆς φυλῆς. Ἀθήνησιν, 1846.

Διήγησις συμβάντων τῆς [As told to Georgios Tertsetes].

Theodoros Kolokotrones, also known as "the old man of the Morea" (Ὁ γέρος τοῦ Μοριᾶ) belonged to an old family of Klephts from Messenia in the Peloponnese. When Theodoros was still a young boy, his father, Konstantinos and two of his uncles were killed by the Turks. Theodoros' mother then took her children to live with her family. When he was old enough, Theodoros Kolokotrones became a Klepht like his father and other members of the Kolokotrones clan. As early as 1802, his exploits against the Turks were becoming known throughout the Peloponnese.

The Turks were able to deplete the ranks of the Klephts in the assaults of 1804–1807, but Kolokotrones was able to escape to Zakynthos, where he procured a small ship, outfitted it and fought in the Aegean under the Russian navy which was at the time engaged in maneuvers against the Turks. It was also during his stay in Zakynthos that Kolokotrones, after the British occupation of the Ionian Islands, joined in 1810 the Duke of York's Greek light infantry which was commanded by major Richard Church. While still

in Zakynthos in 1818 he became a member of the Philike Hetairia. He returned to Mani in the Peloponnese in January 1821 where he assembled forces and on March 23, 1821 heading a complement of Maniotes, he freed the town of Kalamata. During the Greek War of Independence Kolokotrones was in charge of the forces fighting in the Peloponnese. His exploits against the enemy became legendary. After the struggle was over, Kolokotrones was a supporter of Count Ioannes Kapodistrias, who became the first president of Greece and was assassinated in 1831. Because of his opposition to the Bavarian regency he was caught, tried, and condemned to death on June 7, 1834, but was later reprieved. He died in Athens on February 15, 1843.

Kolokotrones' memoirs were dictated to the writer Georgios Tertsetes (1800–1987) in 1836 and were printed in 1846, but did not circulate until 1851.

(1887–Bequest of Professor E. A. Sophocles.

47. Claude Charles Fauriel, 1772–1844. *Chants populaires de la Grèce moderne . . .* avec une traduction française.   Paris, Chez Firmin Didot, Père et fils, 1824–25. 2v.

48. ————. *Prostonarodnyia pesni nyneshnikh grekov . . .* Sanktpeterburg, V tipografii Nikolaia Grecha, 1825.

Although Fauriel was the first to publish a collection of Greek folk songs, he was not the first to show an interest in Greek oral literature. Others before him had made attempts to collect Greek folk songs. As early as 1804 the Swiss Charles Léonard de Sismondi on a trip to Italy had met Andreas Moustoxydis from Corfu, then studying in Pavia, and it seems Moustoxydis promised to send him a collection of songs in modern Greek. However, nothing came of this project. Another serious collector of Greek oral literature was Baron Werner von Haxthausen, who had already gathered and published a collection of German folksongs. In Vienna in 1814 Haxthausen began lessons in modern Greek with Theodoros Manouses, who also helped him to collect Greek songs and to make contacts with the Greeks of Vienna. By the middle of 1815 Haxthausen had collected and translated some fifty Greek songs. Haxthausen had shown some of the songs in his collection to Jacob Grimm and to Goethe, who showed enthusiasm about the project. Nevertheless, the Haxthausen collection remained unpublished until 1935.

Meanwhile, the outbreak of the Greek War of Independence in 1821 put Greece in the forefront of the news in Europe and gave impetus to the project of Claude Fauriel, who with the help of Andreas Moustoxydis was able to collect from the Greeks of Venice and Trieste folk songs which he published in 1824–1825 in two volumes. The Fauriel collection was an instant success and was translated into English by Charles Brinsley Sheridan (1796–1843) in 1825 with the profits to be given to the Society for the Promotion of Greek Education in Greece. A translation of volume one of the Fauriel collection into Russian by Nikolai Ivanovich Gnedich (1784–1835) appeared in Saint Petersburg in 1825.

Following the success of the Fauriel publication other collections of Greek oral poetry appeared in Germany: those by Carl Iken in 1825, P.M.L. Joss in 1826, and Theodor Kind in 1827. All these collections contained songs gathered from the Greeks of the Diaspora. A collection in Russian translation also appeared in 1846, compiled by a Greek, Georgios Evlampios.

It was not until the 1850's that collections of Greek folk poetry appeared closer to home and were gathered from Greece proper and the Ionian Islands. The first was published by Antonios Manousos in 1850 and two years later it was followed by that of Spyridon Zambelios. Both of these collections were printed in Corfu.

Early acquisition – Source unknown.
1884 – Minot Fund.

49. Dionysios Solomos, 1798–1857. Συλλογὴ τῶν γνωστῶν ποιημάτων. Ἐν Ζακύνθῳ, Τυπ. ὁ Ζάκυνθος 1857.

50. ————. Τὰ εὑρισκόμενα Ἐν Κερκύρᾳ, Τυπ. Ἑρμῆς, Ἀντωνίου Τερζάκη 1859.

Dionysios Solomos was born in the Ionian Island of Zakynthos on April 8, 1798. His father, Nikolaos Solomos, was a member of one of the aristocratic families in the island while his mother, Angelike Nikli, was a servant in his father's house. In Zakynthos Solomos studied with the Italian priest Don Santo Rossi who was an exile from Italy because of his liberal ideas. He also studied with Nikolaos Kasimatis and perhaps with Antonios Martelaos. At the age of ten Solomos was sent to Italy to complete his studies, accompanied by his tutor Don Santo Rossi. He studied at the Lyceum of Cremona and then entered the University of Pavia. During the years of his study in Italy, Solomos became acquainted with the poets and litterati of his time and became friends with the poet Vincenzo Monti and the critic Giuseppe Montani. His first poems were written in Italian. He wrote a long poem entitled *La distruzione di Gerusalemme*, and an *Ode per prima messa*, and some sonnets. He returned to Zakynthos in 1818 at the age of twenty.

The ambiance in Zakynthos at the time of Solomos

Салдатъ Греческой
КЛЕФТЪ

ПРОСТОНАРОДНЫЯ

ПѢСНИ

НЫНѢШНИХЪ ГРЕКОВЪ,

СЪ ПОДЛИННИКОМЪ

ИЗДАННЫЯ И ПЕРЕВЕДЕННЫЯ ВЪ СТИХАХЪ, СЪ ПРИБАВЛЕНІЕМЪ
ВВЕДЕНІЯ, СРАВНЕНІЯ ИХЪ СЪ ПРОСТОНАРОДНЫМИ ПѢСНЯМИ
РУСКИМИ И ПРИМѢЧАНІЙ

Н. ГНѢДИЧЕМЪ.

СAНКТПЕТЕРБУРГЪ,

ВЪ ТИПОГРАФІИ НИКОЛАЯ ГРЕЧА.
1825.

48

was not much different from a small town in Northern Italy for there were many Zantiotes who had studied in Italy. Solomos became a member of the group. In their gatherings they would compose impromptu sonnets in Italian. Some of Solomos' sonnets were published in Corfu in 1822 in a collection entitled *Rime improvvisate*. Solomos also wrote a poem in Italian on the death of Ugo Foscolo and delivered the funeral oration in the Catholic church in Zakynthos.

After Solomos returned to Zakynthos, he began to become reacquainted with his mother tongue and began to write in modern Greek. His purpose, to become a Greek poet instead of an Italian one, was reinforced after his meeting with Spyridon Trikoupis (1788–1873) who had gone to Zakynthos at the end of 1822 to await the arrival of Lord Byron. Trikoupis, a relative of Alexandros Mavrokordatos, met Solomos and urged him to write his poetry in Greek because Greece needed poetry and was "waiting for her

Dante." During this first period (1818–1823) Solomos wrote short poems such as the Ἀγνώριστη, Ξανθούλα, Τρελλὴ μάνα and others. He was profoundly moved by the outbreak of the Greek Revolution in 1821 and in 1823 wrote his famous *Hymn to Liberty* (Ὕμνος εἰς τὴν ἐλευθερίαν) a long poem (158 stanzas) inspired by the early events of the Revolution. The work was first published in Missolonghi in 1825. The *Hymn to Liberty* was translated immediately (1825) in English, French and Italian and subsequently into many other languages. In 1824 Solomos wrote an ode *On the Death of Lord Byron* (Εἰς τὸν θάνατον τοῦ Λόρδ Μπάϊρον). During this period he also wrote one of his shortest and most famous poems, occasioned by the destruction of the island of Psara (1825). He composed Ἡ φαρμακωμένη the following year.

In 1828 Solomos went to live in Corfu where he remained until his death in February of 1857. It was in

Corfu that Solomos met the composer Nikolaos Mantzaros with whom he became friends. The first stanzas of the *Hymn to Liberty* set to music by Mantzaros became the Greek national anthem. It was in Corfu that he wrote his most mature works, such as *The Cretan* ('Ο Κρητικός, 1833–1834), *The Free Besieged* ('Ελεύθεροι πολιορκημένοι 1834–1844) about the heroic resistance of Missolonghi, and Πόρφυρας (1849). These three works were never completed and remained in fragmentary form. Toward the end of his life he also wrote some poems in Italian, some of which were written for specific occasions.

Solomos shunned publicity and was reluctant to publish his work. It was not until after his death that most of his output came to light. His complete works were published in Corfu in 1859, compiled and edited from his manuscripts by his close friend, the writer Iakovos Polylas (1829–1896).

In addition to his poetry Solomos wrote Διάλογος, a philosophical work in which he expresses his thoughts about the Greek language and in which he champions the demotic. Solomos' decision to write in the demotic marked a turning point in Greek poetry.

1868–The gift of the family of Cornelius Conway Felton (HC 1827), late President of Harvard College
1964–C. T. Keller Fund.

51. Andreas Kalvos, 1792–1869. *Odes nouvelles de Kalvos de Zante, suivies d'un choix de poésies de Chrestopoulo.* A Paris, Chez Jules Renouard, 1826.

Andreas Kalvos was born on the island of Zakynthos in 1792. Kalvos spent part of his years growing up abroad with his father, who was in Livorno but who also moved frequently from place to place. This made it difficult for the young Kalvos to receive a proper education and he was virtually self taught. In 1812 he had the good fortune to meet the great Italian poet Ugo Foscolo, born also in Zakynthos but of an Italian father and a Greek mother. He served Foscolo as secretary for eight years, followed him into exile in Switzerland and later travelled with him to England.

Kalvos remained in England where he earned a living by teaching Italian and Greek and by translating religious texts into Greek or Italian for a religious society. While in England he gave two public lectures on the relationship between ancient and modern Greek that were well received by the *Times* and the *New Times*. Like Solomos, his first works were written in Italian. He composed the tragedies *Ippia, Teramene*, and *Le Danaidi* and an *Ode agli Ionii*. In 1820 he returned to Florence and spent the winter there, but in April of 1821 he was accused of having secret dealings with the *Carbonari* and was expelled from the city. He went to Geneva where he earned a living by teaching privately.

It was in Geneva that Kalvos published one of the two collections of poetry he wrote in Greek. This was 'Η λύρα (1824) consisting of ten patriotic odes. Eight are about events of the Greek Revolution. Of the remaining two, one is an ode to his native Zakynthos entitled 'Ο φιλόπατρις and the other, Εἰς θάνατον is a recollection of his dead mother. In 1826 another ten lyrics were published in Paris. This volume also includes a selection of poetry by Athanasios Christopoulos (1772–1847) from Kastoria, and French prose translations by Jean Pierre Guillaume Pauthier de Censay. These two slim volumes are the only Greek works of Andreas Kalvos except for an *Ode to Napoleon* ('Ωδὴ στὸ Ναπολέοντα) which he wrote when he was nineteen years old.

In 1826 Kalvos returned to the Ionian Islands via Hydra and Nauplia. He lived in Corfu from 1826 to 1852 and taught both privately and at the Ionian Academy. He returned to England in 1852 where he married Charlotte Augusta Wadams in Louth, Linconshire. He joined his wife in running a school for girls in Linconshire and died there in 1869. In 1960 his remains were transferred and buried with great honor in Zakynthos.

Early acquisition–Source unknown.

52. Ἰόνιος Ἀνθολογία. *Ionian Anthology.* Antologia Ionia. Κέρκυρα, 1834.

In the Ionian Islands, the only part of Greece which did not experience the long years of Turkish Occupation, newspapers and journals were published much earlier than in Greece proper. It was not until the Ionian Islands passed from the Venetians to the French in 1797 that printing came to the islands. The

French established a press on Corfu in 1798 which printed mostly documents and proclamations in Italian, French and Greek, although occasionally it was possible to print pamphlets and other materials of a different nature. The Ionian Islands passed through various hands frequently during this period, but there was always some forms of printing in Corfu and later in Zakynthos, nearly always of an official nature. However, from 1803 on newspapers and journals began to make their appearance. These were usually published in Italian and Greek, for Italian was the official language of the islands for centuries during the Venetian period.

In 1834 when the Ἰόνιος Ἀνθολογία began publication the Ionian Islands were under British rule. Thus, besides Greek and Italian, English was added to the "official" languages of the islands. It is interesting to note that it was not until 1852 that the Greek language became the national language of the Ionian Islands. The Ἰόνιος Ἀνθολογία was inaugurated under the patronage of the Governor General of the islands, George Grenville, Lord Nugent. In the first issue of the journal an excerpt from the poem Λάμπρος of Dionysios Solomos was published anonymously for the first time. It appears that Lady Nugent herself had asked Dionysios Solomos for one of his works to appear in the inaugural issue of the journal. During the brief period of its existence, the Ἰόνιος Ἀνθολογία enjoyed a great reputation.

1868–The gift of the family of Cornelius Conway Felton (HC 1827) late President of Harvard College. Inscribed "C. C. Felton from his friend I or J. F."

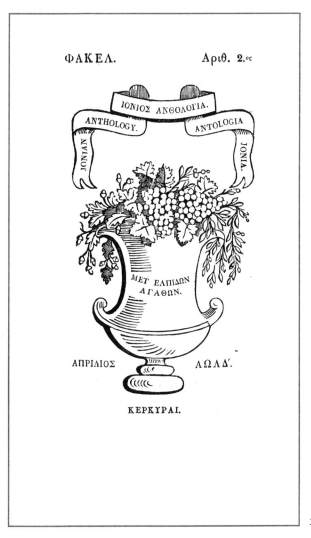

52

53. Andreas Laskaratos, 1811–1901. *Τὰ μυστήρια τῆς Κεφαλονιᾶς. Ἐν Κεφαληνίᾳ, Ἐκ τοῦ τυπολραφείου ἡ Κεφαληνία, 1856.*

Andreas Laskaratos was born in the town of Lixouri in Cephalonia. After he finished the Guilford Lyceum in Cephalonia, where he was a pupil of Neophytos Vamvas, he entered the Ionian Academy in Corfu and studied with Andreas Kalvos, among others. He subsequently studied law in France and Italy and got his law degree from the Universtiy of Pisa in 1846. He practiced law in Lixouri but he gave that up in order to devote himself to writing. Laskaratos' satirical vein got him into trouble after the publication of *Τὰ μυστήρια τῆς Κεφαλονιᾶς* in 1856, in which he satirizes the Cephalonian mode of life. The work is divided into three sections: Home Life, Religion, and Politics. The work created a sensation among the Cephalonians, especially his opinions about illiteracy

and superstition among the clergy. On March 2, 1856 he was excommunicated by the Church and life became so difficult for him that he was forced to move to nearby Zakynthos and eventually went to London, where he taught Greek and Italian to provide himself a livelihood. He returned to Cephalonia in 1859 and published the satirical newspaper *Λύχνος*. In 1900, one year before his death, the excommunication was lifted.

1868–The gift of the family of Cornelius Conway Felton (HC 1827) late President of Harvard College. On the titlepage there is the following dedication in Greek: "To Professor Felton a token of respect" The Author.

ΤΑ

ΜΥΣΤΗΡΙΑ ΤΗΣ ΚΕΦΑΛΟΝΙΑΣ

Η

ΣΚΕΨΕΣ ΑΠΑΝΟΥ ΣΤΗΝ ΟΙΚΟΓΕΝΕΙΑ ΣΤΗ
ΘΡΗΣΚΙΑ ΚΑΙ ΣΤΗΝ ΠΟΛΙΤΙΚΗ
ΕΙΣ ΤΗΝ ΚΕΦΑΛΟΝΙΑ.

Andreas Laskaratos.
ΠΑΡΑ ΤΟΥ ΚΥΡΙΟΥ ΑΝΔ. ΛΑΣΚΑΡΑΤΟΥ.

Οὐδὲν συνκεκαλυμένον ἐστὶν, ὃ οὐκ
ἀποκαλυφθήσεται· καὶ κρυπτὸν ὃ οὐ
γνωσθήσεται.

Εὐαγ. κατὰ Λουκᾶν. Κεφ. 12.

ΕΝ ΚΕΦΑΛΗΝΙΑ.
ΕΚ ΤΟΥ ΤΥΠΟΓΡΑΦΕΙΟΥ Η «ΚΕΦΑΛΗΝΙΑ»

1856.

53

ΚΩΣΤΗ ΠΑΛΑΜΑ

ΤΡΑΓΟΥΔΙΑ

ΤΗΣ ΠΑΤΡΙΔΟΣ ΜΟΥ

ΤΡΑΓΟΥΔΙΑ ΤΗΣ ΛΙΜΝΗΣ
ΤΡΑΓΟΥΔΙΑ ΤΗΣ ΚΑΡΔΙΑΣ ΚΑΙ ΤΗΣ ΖΩΗΣ
ΠΟΛΕΜΙΚΑ ΤΡΑΓΟΥΔΙΑ

ΕΝ ΑΘΗΝΑΙΣ
1886

54

54. Kostes Palamas, 1859–1943.   *Τραγούδια τῆς πατρίδος μου.*
Ἐν Ἀθήναις, 1886.

55. ——— . *A Hundred Voices and Other Poems from the Second Part of "Life Immovable".*   Translated with an Introduction and Notes by Aristides E. Phoutrides. Cambridge, Harvard University Press, 1921.

Kostes Palamas was born in Patras of a family from Missolonghi. His father was a magistrate. He lost both his parents when he was very young and he was brought up by his paternal uncle in Missolonghi where he completed his primary and secondary education. In 1875 he entered the School of Law of the University of Athens. During his student years and later Palamas was active in writing articles in various journals and newspapers. This became a means of earning his living. In 1897 he was appointed General Secretary of the University of Athens, a post he held for some thirty years. In 1930 he became the President of the Academy of Athens.

Palamas started writing poetry at an early age. In Athens, even though he was studying law, he soon became involved in the intellectual and literary life of the city. This necessitated that he take part in the language controversy between the purists who favored the use of the *katharevousa* and the demoticists who wanted literature to be written in the spoken language.

Unlike the literary exponents of the Ionian School which favored the demotic, at the time Palamas went to Athens the purists reigned supreme. They dominated just about everything, the newspapers and literary journals, as well as the committees at the university that judged the literary competitions. Although Palamas' early poems were written in *katharevousa* he was soon writing in the demotic and became the chief literary exponent of the demoticist movement. Palamas was convinced that the demotic should become the universal language for literature and towards this end he directed his considerable talents.

His reputation as a poet and the champion of the demoticists was already in full force when he published his first collection of poetry, *Τραγούδια τῆς πατρίδος μου* in 1886. Palamas was a prolific writer. He published many volumes of poetry as well as two short stories and one play. He also wrote a great number of articles in newspapers and journals. His most important poems are *Ὁ δωδεκάλογος τοῦ γύφτου* (1907) and *Ἡ φλογέρα τοῦ Βασιλιᾶ* (1910).

The first translations of Palamas into English were made in 1919 by a young Greek classicist, Aristides Phoutrides, who was born on the island of Ikaria and was trained at Harvard. He also taught at both Harvard and Yale before his untimely death in 1923.

Περιμένοντας τους Βαρβάρους.

— Τι περιμένουμε στην αγορά συναθροισμένοι;
  Είναι οι βάρβαροι να φθάσουν σήμερα.

— Γιατί μέσα στην Σύγκλητο μια τέτοια απραξία;
  Τι κάθοντ' οι Συγκλητικοί και δεν νομοθετούνε;

  Γιατί οι βάρβαροι θα φθάσουν σήμερα.
  Τι νόμους πια θα κάμουν οι Συγκλητικοί;
  Οι βάρβαροι σαν έλθουν θα νομοθετήσουν.

— Γιατί ο αυτοκράτωρ μας τόσο πρωί σηκώθη,
  και κάθεται στης πόλεως την πιο μεγάλη πύλη
  στον θρόνο επάνω, επίσημος, φορώντας την κορώνα;

  Γιατί οι βάρβαροι θα φθάσουν σήμερα
  Κι ο αυτοκράτωρ περιμένει να δεχθεί

τον αρχηγό τους. Μάλιστα ετοίμασε
για να τον δώσει μια περγαμηνή. Εκεί
τον έγραψε τίτλους πολλούς κι ονόματα.

— Γιατί οι δυο μας ύπατοι κ' οι πραίτορες εβγήκαν
σήμερα με τες κόκκινες, τες κεντημένες τόγες·
γιατί βραχιόλια φόρεσαν με τόσους αμεθύστους,
και δαχτυλίδια με λαμπρά γυαλιστερά σμαράγδια·
γιατί να πιάσουν σήμερα πολύτιμα μπαστούνια
μ' ασήμια και μαλάματα έκτακτα σκαλισμένα;

  Γιατί οι βάρβαροι θα φθάσουν σήμερα·
  και τέτοια πράγματα θαμπώνουν τους βαρβάρους.

— Γιατί κ' οι άξιοι ρήτορες δεν έρχονται σαν πάντα
να βγάλουνε τους λόγους τους, να πούνε τα δικά τους;

  Γιατί οι βάρβαροι θα φθάσουν σήμερα·
  κι αυτοί βαρυούντ' ευφράδειες και δημηγορίες.

— Γιατί ν' αρχίσει μονομιάς αυτή η ανησυχία
κ' η σύγχυσις. (Τα πρόσωπα τι σοβαρά που εγίναν).
Γιατί αδειάζουν γρήγορα οι δρόμοι κ' η πλατέες,

κι όλοι γυρνούν στα σπίτια τους πολύ συλλογισμένοι;

  Γιατί ενύχτωσε κ' οι βάρβαροι δεν ήλθαν.
  Και μερικοί έφθασαν απ' τα σύνορα,
  και είπανε πως βάρβαροι πια δεν υπάρχουν.

Και τώρα τι θα γένουμε χωρίς βαρβάρους.
Οι άνθρωποι αυτοί ήσαν μια κάποια λύσις.

Phoutrides was an enemy of the demotic movement during the linguistic controversy but later became an ardent disciple of Palamas. His first translation of Palamas' Ἡ ἀσάλευτηζωή in two volumes, was brought out by the Harvard University Press, the second volume under the title *A Hundred Voices* (1921). He also translated Palamas' only play Ἡ τρισεύγενη published by Yale University Press in 1923 under the title *Royal Blossom*.

Palamas was the first Greek poet to be nominated for the Nobel Prize in literature. Romain Rolland, who nominated him in 1930, called him the greatest living poet in Europe.

1897 – Subscription Fund.
1929 – Professor Albert Andrew Howard.

56. C. P. Cavafy, 1863–1933.   Ms.   *Ποιήματα*.   Ἀλεξάνδρεια 1917.

57. ———.   *Ποιήματα*.   Ἀλεξάνδρεια 1935.

C. P. Cavafy (Κωνσταντῖνος Π. Καβάφης) was born in Alexandria, Egypt of parents who came from Constantinople. His father was a businessman who ran the largest and most successful export-import firm in Egypt, with branches in London, Liverpool, Manchester, Marseilles and Constantinople. During his early years Constantine grew up in luxury with a French tutor and an English nurse and many servants. However, his father's death in 1870 left the family in straitened circumstances. In 1872 his mother moved the family to Liverpool, where there was a branch of the family business. He also spent some time in London during this period. He later spent three years in Constantinople with his mother's family. By 1885 the family was back in Alexandria and there Cavafy remained for the rest of his life except for a few brief trips to Athens and equally brief stays in London and Paris. Cavafy worked in the Department of Irrigation of the Ministry of Public Works until his retirement in 1922. After his retirement he dedicated himself entirely to poetry until his death in 1933.

Cavafy's poetry first appeared in 1886. However, he discarded most of his very early poetry and considered the year 1891 as the beginning of his poetic expression. It was in 1891 that he printed a broadsheet of his poem Κτίσται in Alexandria. Other of his early poems were subsequently published in pamphlet form. Cavafy had them printed and distributed to close friends. From time to time beginning with 1904, he would have twelve or more printed together. The small collections entitled *Ποιήματα* were printed in very limited editions.

Cavafy himself considered that it was not until 1911 that he found his true voice. Often, even during his later years, he discarded poems he did not want included in the corpus of poems he recognized. The total number of poems he approved was 154. He was a perfectionist and he constantly reworked and discarded. Except for some contributions to journals his poems were not published during his lifetime except for what he himself had privately printed and distributed. Cavafy never offered his poetry for sale.

Two years after his death, his heir Alekos Senkopoulos published the 154 poems in a first collected edition. Later other poems were found among his papers, perhaps to be revised and published later or to be discarded. These unpublished poems came to light after 1948 and in 1968, under the editorship of G. P. Savvidis, seventy-five of the poems written between 1882 and 1923 appeared under the title Ἀνέκδοτα ποιήματα.

1978 – The gift of Professor George P. Savvidis.
1939 – The gift of Professor Raphael Demos (HU Ph.D. 1916)

58. Angelos Sikelianos, 1884–1951.   Ἀλαφροΐσκιωτος.   Ἐν Ἀθήναις, Τύποις Π. Δ. Σακελλαρίου 1909.

59. ———.   *Πρόλογος στὴ ζωή*.   [Ἀθήνα, 1915–1917] 4 vols.

Angelos Sikelianos was born on the Ionian island of Leukas. The Ionian Islands had a strong demotic tradition characterized by a deep feeling for the modern Greek language and a familiarity with foreign literature, especially that of Italy. During his early years Sikelianos travelled extensively throughout Greece and was able to absorb the landscape, history, and traditions which are expressed in his first major

Κ.Π.ΚΑΒΑΦΗ
ΠΟΙΗΜΑΤΑ

ΚΑΛΛΙΤΕΧΝΙΚΗ ΕΡΓΑΣΙΑ ΤΑΚΗ ΚΑΛΜΟΥΧΟΥ.
ΦΙΛΟΛΟΓΙΚΗ ΕΠΙΜΕΛΕΙΑ ΡΙΚΑΣ ΣΕΓΚΟΠΟΥΛΟΥ.
ΜΕΡΙΜΝΑ ΕΝΩΣΕΩΣ "ΕΛΛΗΝΩΝ ΛΟΓΟΤΕΧΝΩΝ.
ΕΚΔΟΣΙΣ "ΑΛΕΞΑΝΔΡΙΝΗΣ ΤΕΧΝΗΣ.
10, RUE LEPSIUS, ALEXANDRIE – ÉGYPTE.

work, the Ἀλαφροΐσκιωτος written in 1907 and printed privately two years later. The title of this work was taken from a line in Dionysios Solomos' *Free Besieged* (Ἐλεύθεροι πολιορκημένοι). This quasi-autobiographical work established Sikelianos as a major literary figure almost overnight.

Sikelianos' sister Penelope had married Raymond Duncan, the brother of Isadora Duncan. It was through his sister that he met the American Eva Palmer whom he married in 1907 at Bar Harbor, Maine. Sikelianos and his wife attempted to organize an international Delphic center and a Delphic university. In 1927 and 1930 they financed and organized a Delphic Festival which had productions of theatrical works, among them Aeschylus' *Prometheus Bound* and *The Suppliants*. Dance productions, craft exhibitions, and athletic games were also part of the festival. Although the Academy of Athens cited Eva and Angelos Sikelianos for this effort, the Delphic idea and the festivals were a financial failure and this was a source of disillusionment for both of them. Eva Sikelianos parted from her husband and returned to the United States in 1933. She did not return to Greece until 1952, the year she died and was buried in Delphi. In 1955 the Council of Europe founded a Pan-European

Delphic Festival in honor of Angelos Sikelianos. Sikelianos died in 1951 in Athens. He had been in poor health for some time when he accidentally drank Lysol instead of his medication.

His work includes nine books of poetry, among them Πρόλογος στὴ ζωή published in four sections between 1915 and 1917: Ἡ συνείδηση τῆς γῆς μου, Ἡ συνείδηση τῆς φυλῆς μου, Ἡ συνείδηση τῆς γυναίκας and Ἡ συνείδηση τῆς πίστης. A fifth part, Ἡ συνείδηση τῆς προσωπικῆς δημιουργίας was not completed until 1947. In 1917 Sikelianos completed his long poem Μήτηρ Θεοῦ published in 1919, and in 1918 Τὸ Πάσχα τῶν Ἑλλήνων which came out in 1922. Other major works include Δελφικὸς λόγος (1927), and Ἱερὰ Ὁδός (1935). Besides his lyrical works which consist of some nine books of poetry, Sikelianos wrote seven poetic dramas among them, Ὁ διθύραμβος τοῦ ρόδου (1932), Ὁ Δαίδαλος στὴν Κρήτη (1943), Σιβύλλα (1944), Ὁ Χριστὸς στὴ Ρώμη (1946), and Ὁ θάνατος τοῦ Διγενῆ (1950).

1980–A. Lowell Fund.
1980–Coolidge Memorial Fund.

60. Nikos Kazantzakis, 1883–1957.   Ὀdýsseia.   Ἀθήνα,Πυρσός, 1938.

Nikos Kazantzakis was born in 1883 in Herakleion, Crete. He earned a degree in law at the University of Athens and later continued his studies at the Sorbonne. He also attended lectures by Henri Bergson at the Collège de France. It was after this period that Kazantzakis began his many wanderings throughout the world. He travelled to and spent some time in Germany, Austria, England, Spain, Russia, China, Italy, Palestine, Egypt, Cyprus, Yugoslavia, Japan, and Czechoslovakia. In order to cover his expenses, at least partially, for his extensive travels, he wrote a series of articles for Greek newspapers. These were later expanded and shaped into travel books. He wrote travelogues on Russia, Spain, Italy, Cyprus, Palestine, Japan and England.

Kazantzakis began his career as a writer in 1906 with a work entitled Ὄφις καὶ κρίνο writing under the pseudonym Κάρμα Νιρβαμή. His early works were for the most part dramas: Ὁ πρωτομάστορας (1910), Νικηφόρος Φωκᾶς (1927), Χριστός (1928), Ὀδυσσέας (1928), Μέλισσα (1939), Ἰουλιανός (1945), Καποδίστριας (1946). Kazantzakis translated a number of works from different languages. He was fluent in French, German, Italian and Spanish and had

a working knowledge of English and Russian. He translated Nietzsche's *Thus Spoke Zarathustra* and *The Birth of Tragedy*, Bergson's *On Laughter*, William James' *Theory of Emotion*, Darwin's *The Origin of Species*, and other works. He also translated into verse Dante's *Divine Comedy* and the first part of Goethe's *Faust*. His most famous translations, however, were his translations into modern Greek of Homer's *Iliad* and *Odyssey*. This was done with the help and collaboration of the Homeric scholar Ioannis Kakrides.

In 1919 Kazantzakis was appointed General Director of the Ministry of Public Welfare by the Venizelos government. His main assignment was to direct the repatriation of about 150,000 Greek refugees from the Caucasus into Thrace and Macedonia. One of his assistants was Yioryis Zorbas who was later to become the main character of his novel Βίος καὶ πολιτεία τοῦ Ἀλέξη Ζορμπᾶ.

Kazantzakis became known abroad through his novels, which have been translated into some twenty languages. Best known among them are *Zorba the Greek*, which was also made into a film and had a very successful stage run on Broadway. Another novel, *The Greek Passion*, (Ὁ Χριστὸς

ξανασταυρώνεται) was staged as a play in Athens and at the Yale Drama School and made into a film. It was also set to music in an opera by Bohuslav Martinu. His novel *Freedom or Death* (Ὁ Καπετὰν Μιχάλης) was produced as a play in Athens and set to music by Manos Hadzidakis. Some of his plays, Μέλισσα, Ἰουλιανὸς ὁ Παραβάτης and Καποδίστριας were produced in Greece.

While he was in Crete in 1924 Kazantzakis began working on his major work, the long epic poem Ὀδύσσεια (33,333 verses). He worked and reworked it during a seven year period. It was first published in 1935 in Athens in an edition of 300 copies. The *Odyssey* of Nikos Kazantzakis has been characterized by some critics as the most ambitious literary accomplishment of the twentieth century. However, as

with everything Kazantzakis did and wrote, the publication of the *Odyssey* did not bring praise only. Some critics attacked the work and rejected it. Perhaps one of the reasons was that Kazantzakis had dared to write a sequel to Homer's *Odyssey*.

Even Kazantzakis' death and burial were controversial. The Archbishop of Athens refused permission for his body to lie in state in Athens. However, the Church of Crete, being autonomous, gave him a hero's funeral. He was buried on the bastion of the Venetian fortress of Herakleion. Kazantzakis was nominated for the Nobel Prize in literature by Albert Schweitzer and Thomas Mann.

1979 – The gift of Eleni N. Kazantzakis.

61. George Seferis, 1900 – 1971. Ἡμερολόγιο καταστρώματος. Ἀθήνα, 1940.

62. ———. Ἥ συνομιλία μέ τόν Φαβρίκιο. Ms. Ἀθήνα, 1966.

Yiorgos Seferis was the pseudonym of Georgios Sepheriades. He was born in Smyrna (Izmir, Turkey) and spent the first fourteen years of his life there. When the First World War broke out in 1914 the family moved to Greece and settled in Athens. His father Stylianos Sepheriades was Professor of International Law at the University of Athens. After completion of his secondary education Seferis went to France to study law at the University of Paris. In 1926, upon his return to Greece, he was appointed to the Ministry of Foreign Affairs. He spent most of his career in the diplomatic service where he held a variety of posts in many parts of the world. His last post before retirement in 1962 was as Ambassador to Great Britain. He settled in Athens in 1963 and died there in 1971.

Sepheris' first book of poetry, Στροφή (*Turning Point*), appeared in 1931 and was followed by Ἥ στέρνα (*The Cistern*) 1932, and Μυθιστόρημα (*Myth of Our History*) in 1935. Other poetry collections include Ἡμερολόγιο καταστρωώματος (*Logbook I*, 1940) and Τετράδιο γθμνασμάτων, 1940. ᾽ Ἡμερολόγιο καταστρώματος II, first appeared in Alexandria, Egypt in 1945, where Seferis was with the Greek government in exile during the Occupation of Greece by the Germans. The poems in this collection were all written in various parts of the world where Seferis went as a representative of the Greek government. The poem Κίχλη (*Thrush*) appeared in

1947. It was written during Seferis' stay on the island of Poros and the name "thrush" is the name of a boat sunk by the Germans which remained submerged in the small harbor of Poros. *Thrush* is considered by many to be Sepheris' most personal poem. The ten years which followed were spent in various posts outside Greece, in Ankara, Beirut and London. During this period he visited the monasteries of Cappadocia and also went to Cyprus. In 1955 he published a collection of his Cyprus poems with the title . . . Κύπρον, οὗ μ' ἐθέσπισεν . . . The title is taken from a line in Euripides. They were later reprinted as Ἡμερολόγιο καταστρώματος III. The impressions of his travels to the monasteries of Cappadocia resulted in a book, *Trois jours dans les églises rupestres de Cappadoce* (1953), which appeared simultaneously in French and Greek editions. The last poetry collection was his Τρία κρυφὰ ποιήματα (*Three Secrets Poems*) which appeared in 1966. His last poem Οἱ γάτες τ᾽ Ἄη Νικόλα (*The Cats of Saint Nicholas*) was privately printed in 1969. It appeared in the anthology Δεκαοκτὼ κείμενα (*Eighteen Texts*) in 1970. A collection of essays Δοκιμές appeared in a book in 1944 and in 1962 came out in an enlarged edition. Some of his essays appeared in English as *On the Greek Style* in 1966. A travel book Δελφοί appeared in 1962. Ἡ συνομιλία μέ τὸν Φαβρίκιο was written in November 1966 and is a reminiscence of his friend, the writer Yiorgos

62

Theotokas (1906–1966), who had just died. It was published in the January 1967 issue of the journal Ἐποχές. The correspondence between Seferis and Yiorgos Theotokas entitled Ἀλληλογραφία (1930–1966) was published in 1975.

Besides his poetry and prose Seferis translated T. S. Eliot's *The Waste Land and Other Poems* and *Murder in the Cathedral*. He also translated poetry by Ezra Pound, W. B. Yeats, Archibald MacLeish, W. H. Auden, Marianne Moore, André Gide and others. He also translated into modern Greek *The Song of Songs* and *The Apocalypse* of Saint John.

Seferis received many honors and distinctions. They include honorary degrees from Oxford, Cambridge, the University of Thessaloniki and Princeton. He was elected Honorary Foreign Member of the American Academy of Arts and Sciences. He received the Palamas Award in Athens in 1947, The William Foyle Prize in Poetry in London in 1961 and in 1963 the Nobel Prize for literature.

1959–Susan A.E. Morse Fund.
1974–The gift of Mrs. Maro Seferis.

En Harvard Library
George Seferis

ΓΙΩΡΓΟΣ ΣΕΦΕΡΗΣ

ΟΙ ΓΑΤΕΣ Τ' ΑΗ ΝΙΚΟΛΑ

ΑΘΗΝΑ

63. Yannis Ritsos, 1909 –   *Πέτρες, Ἐπαναλήψεις, Κιγκλίδωμα.* *Ἀθήνα, Κέδρος,* 1972.

Yannis Ritsos was born in the medieval fortress town of Monemvasia in the Peloponnese. His father was a landowner who was ruined after the Asia Minor catastrophe. After completing his secondary education Ritsos went to Athens in 1925 and enrolled at the University of Athens. In order to earn his living at a time when Athens was flooded with refugees from Anatolia, he held jobs as typist, clerk for a notary public and calligrapher for law diplomas. Before he was able to complete his studies Ritsos fell ill with tuberculosis and had to spend several years in a sanatorium in Athens and then in Crete. Both his mother and elder brother had died of tuberculosis and his father died in an insane asylum. His sister also spent some years there.

Because of his poor health and his commitment to Marxism Ritsos' life was full of tragic events. In 1936 during the Metaxas dictatorship, Ritsos' poem

ΓΙΑΝΝΗΣ ΡΙΤΣΟΣ

ΠΕΤΡΕΣ
ΕΠΑΝΑΛΗΨΕΙΣ
ΚΙΓΚΛΙΔΩΜΑ

ΚΕΔΡΟΣ - 1972

Ἐπιτάφιος, a lament of a mother for her son killed by the army and the police during a worker's strike, was burnt along with other books in front of the Temple of Zeus in Athens. During the German-Italian Occupation of Greece Ritsos joined the Resistance movement and became a member of EDA (Union of Democratic Left). In 1944, after the collapse of the Left, Ritsos went into hiding. He was arrested in 1948 and spent time in various detention camps on the islands of Lemnos and Makronisos and Saint Efstratios (Ai Stratis) between 1948 and 1952. During this four year period of incarceration Ritsos continued to write. Although Ritsos had not taken active part in any political affairs after his release, when the junta took over in 1967 Ritsos was again arrested and sent to a detention camp on the island of Yaros and then to Leros. During this time his health deteriorated and he had to be hospitalized again. Because of great pressure from abroad — there were petitions by a great number of writers and artists, among them Picasso, Gunter Grass, Arthur Miller, Pablo Neruda, Sartre, Rostropovich and many others — the junta government offered to release him under certain conditions in 1970 but Ritsos felt he could not accept the conditions. He was permitted to live in exile in a village on the island of Samos where his wife was able to join him. After the fall of the junta Ritsos returned to his home in Athens and since then he has been able to write and live his life without restrictions.

In 1956 he was awarded the National Prize for poetry for his collection Ἡ σονάτα τοῦ σεληνόφωτος. The prize gained him recognition outside Greece. When the collection of his poetry was translated into French, Louis Aragon hailed him as one of the greatest and most original contemporary poets. In 1975 the University of Thessaloniki conferred on him the Honorary Degree of Doctor of Philosophy. No other Greek poet has received as many honors and awards as Yannis Ritsos. His many awards include the Grand International Prize of the Biennale of Poetry at Krokkele-Zout, Belgium, 1972; Membership at the Academy of Science and Literature, Mainz, West Germany, 1972; The "Alfred de Vigny" award in poetry, Paris, 1975; two poetry awards from Italy in 1976; the Lenin Prize, Moscow, 1977; the International Prize for poetry, Mondello, Italy, 1978; an honorary degree from the University of Birmingham, 1978; the International Peace Prize for Culture from the World Peace Council, 1979. He has been nominated several times for the Nobel Prize in literature.

Ritsos is a prolific poet with over a hundred poetry collections to his credit. He has also translated into modern Greek works by such authors as Vladimir Mayakovsky, Nazim Hikmet, Ilya Ehrenburg, Jorge Guillèn and also published anthologies of Rumanian and Czech poetry. Ritsos is also an accomplished painter. During the years of his exile he managed to work with whatever materials he could find, paper, pebbles, stone, glass and wood. Often his poetry collections are illustrated, as in the present case, with reproductions of his own work.

1987 – The gift of Evro Layton (RI 1970)

64. Odysseas Elytis, 1911 – Τό ἄξιον ἐστί. Ἀθῆναι, Ἐκδοτικὴ Ἑταιρεία Ἴκαρος, 1959.

Odysseas Elytis is the pseudonym of Odysseas Alepoudelis. He was born in 1911 in Herakleion, Crete of a well-known industrial family. Both parents were originally from the island of Lesvos (Mytilene). His father was a soap manufacturer. The family moved to Athens in 1914, where Odysseas went to school. His summers were invariably spent on vacation in different islands of the Aegean. In 1930 he enrolled at the School of Law of the University of Athens. He spent the years 1948–1951 in Paris studying literature at the Sorbonne. During this period he wrote art and literary criticism for the paper Καθημερινή and the French magazine *Verve*. He is himself an accomplished painter and has worked in watercolor, gouache and collage. During this period he also travelled extensively in Europe.

At an early stage in his career as a poet, wanting to dissociate himself from the industrial world he created and used the pseudonym Elytis. His first poems were published in 1935 in the November issue of the new journal Τὰ Νέα Γράμματα a periodical which played an important role especially in poetry but also in all other intellectual manifestations and was the main outlet for what is known as the "Generation of the Thirties". The journal was edited by the critic Antreas Karantones and was closely connected with Giorgos Katsimbalis, the "Colossus of Maroussi" celebrated by Henry Miller, and with the poet George Seferis. Elytis' poetry first appeared in book form in 1940 under the title Προσανατολισμοί (*Orientations*). This first collection contains one of his best known and much translated poems, Ἡ τρελλή ῥοδιά (*The Mad*

ΟΔΥΣΣΕΑ ΕΛΥΤΗ

Λιθογραφία Γιάννη Μόραλη

ΤΟ ΑΞΙΟΝ ΕΣΤΙ

"Ίκαρος" Ἐκδοτικὴ Ἑταιρία

Pomegranate Tree) a poem that is very characteristic of Elytis' early poetry which is exuberant, full of the light of the Aegean and the joy of life. His next collection of poetry appeared in 1943, entitled Ἥλιος ὁ πρῶτος (*Sun the First*).

During World War II Elytis served on the Albanian front as a Second Lieutenant in the Greek infantry. This experience came to manifest itself in his later poetry where one can find a much more somber and mature tone. This is reflected in the long poem he wrote in 1945 and published in 1962, ᾼσμα ἡρωϊκὸ καὶ πένθιμο γιὰ τὸν χαμένο ἀνθυπολοχαγὸ τῆς Ἀλβανίας (*Heroic and Elegiac Song for the Lost Second Lieutenant of the Albanian Campaign*). After writing the *Asma heroïko kai penthimo* and one other work entitled Ἡ καλοσύνη στὶς Λυκοποριές there was a silence of more than ten years before a new work appeared. This was a major work, Τό Ἄξιον Ἐστί (1959) considered to be Elytis' most important work. The title is a phrase which occurs frequently in the Greek Orthodox Liturgy and hymnography. The work is divided into three parts, Ἡ Γένεσις, Τὰ Πάθη, Τὸ Δοξαστικόν. When the work was first published in Greece it was received with caution by Greek critics. One of the first scholars to recognize its importance and write about it was G. P. Savvidis. In 1964 Mikis Theodorakis set to music *The Axion Esti*.

Later collections of poetry include Ἔξη καὶ μιὰ τύψεις γιὰ τὸν οὐρανό, 1960 (*Six and One Remorses for the Sky*), Ὁ ἥλιος ὁ ἡλιάτορας, 1971 (*The Sovereign Sun*), Τὸ ρῶ τοῦ ἔρωτα, 1972, Ὁ φυλλομάντης, 1973, Σηματολόγιον, 1977, Μαρία Νεφέλη, 1978, Τρία ποιήματα μὲ σημαία εὐκαιρίας, 1982, Ἡμερολόγιο ἑνὸς ἀθέατου Ἀπριλίου, 1984. Elytis has also published a book of essays entitled Ἀνοιχτὰ χαρτιά, 1974, a work on the painter Theophilos Chatzemichael (Ὁ ζωγράφος Θεόφιλος, 1973) and a monograph on the short story writer Alexandros Papadiamantes (1851–1911), Ἡ μαγεία τοῦ Παπαδιαμάντη, 1976. He has also translated the poetry of Éluard, Jouve, Lorca, Ungaretti, Rimbaud, Mayakovsky and others. More recently, he brought out (1984) a collection entitled Σαπφώ, ἀνασύνθεση καὶ ἀπόδοση consisting of texts of the poems of Sappho with free renditions into modern Greek. In 1979 he was awarded the Nobel Prize in literature.

1960 – Fund given in memory of Frederic Hilborn Hall (HC 1910).

1.)
The Byzantine double-headed eagle used as the mark of the printer Zacharias Kalliergis in Venice and Rome (1499–1524). Ἐτυμολογικὸν μέγα, 1499.

2.)
The mark of the publisher Nikolaos Vlastos of Crete (1499–1500) who financed the first four works printed by Zacharias Kalliergis. Ἐτυμολογικὸν μέγα, 1499.

3.)
The mark of Andreas Kounadis of Patras. The device is a
marten, in Greek κουνάδι or κουνάβι. Homer. Ἰλιάς.
Venice, 1526.

4.)
The bee, symbol of the firm of Nikolaos Glykys in Venice
(1670–1854) Ψαλτήριον. 1692. Ὀκτώηχος, 1701.
Dorotheos, metropolitan of Monemvasia.
Βιβλίον ἱστορικόν. 1750.

5.)

The double-headed eagle was also used as the printer's mark
of Demetrios and Panos Theodosiou of Ioannina active in
Venice between 1755 and 1824. Harmenopoulos,
Konstantinos. Ἑξάβιβλος. 1777. Ioannou, Manthos.
Στιχολογία. ὡραιοτάτη. 1803.

6.)

The siren (γοργόνα) was the mark of the printer Nikolaos
Saros (Venice 1681–1778). Βιβλίον περιέχον τὴν
᾿Ακολουθίαν τῆς ἁγίας Αἰκατερίνης. 1727.

7.)

The coat of arms of Serapheim Pissidios, metropolitan of Ankara, formerly the Abbot of the Kykko monastery in Cyprus. Βιβλίον καλούμενον Ραντισμοῦ στηλίτευσις. Leipzig, 1758.

8.)

The mark of the Patriarchal press of Constantinople first used in 1798. Augustinus, Aurelius, bp. of Hippo, Ἐπιτομή . . . 1799. Watts, Isaac Τὸ τέλος τοῦ χρόνου. 1818.

Ἰωάννης πα-
λαιολόγ.

Ἐμμανουὴλ ὁ παλαιολ.

Θεόδωρος
ὁ πορφυρο-
γέννητος.

Ἀνδρόνικος
παλαιολόγ.

Ἑλένη παλαιολόγου.

Εἰκόνες τῆς γενεᾶς τῶν παλαιολόγων Αὐτοκρατόρων Ῥωμαίων.